THE
ENCYCLOPEDIA
OF
GRANDPARENTING
Hundreds of Ideas to
Entertain Your Grandchildren

Rosemary Dalton
Peter Dalton

Illustrated by Kathleen Estes

D1041505

BRISTOL PUBLISHING ENTERPRISES, INC.
SAN LEANDRO, CALIFORNIA

Printed in the United States of America.

ISBN 1-55867-004-1

TABLE OF CONTENTS

LOOK FOR THESE TITLES IN OUR
MATURE READER SERIES:

OVER 50 AND STILL COOKING!
Recipes for Good Health and Long Life

THE NUTRITION GAME:
The Right Moves if You're Over 50

THE ENCYCLOPEDIA OF GRANDPARENTING
Hundreds of Ideas to Entertain Your
Grandchildren

DEALS & DISCOUNTS
If You're 50 or Older

**START YOUR OWN BUSINESS
AFTER 50 — OR 60 — OR 70!**
These People Did. Here's How:

I DARE YOU!
How to Stay Young Forever

THE BEGINNER'S ANCESTOR RESEARCH KIT

1. THE GRANDCHILDREN ARE COMING TO VISIT!

Isn't that good news! But your second thought may be, "How will I keep them busy? What is worthwhile but entertaining too?"

WHY YOU MAY NEED HELP

We know you're probably busier than you've ever been, working at a job or as a volunteer or with other personal projects. And it's possible that you are not accustomed to having younger people around the house. Or perhaps you have experience with children, but can use new ideas. So we've developed this book to give you a handy resource full of ideas to fit a variety of circumstances, and make the kids' stay a pleasure for all of you.

Some of our suggestions are for quiet activities that the youngsters can pursue while you go about tasks that you must do without much interruption. Many activities are suggested for you to do *with* your grandchildren, because the time you spend together is so valuable for all of you. Some activities are short, some more complicated. Many are inexpensive and can be done with items you already have.

STRENGTHEN YOUR TIES

Most important, we think the activities we have provided for you will help you become wonderful friends with your grandchildren, and will help them remember you and the time they spent with you with great fondness. This is one of the best legacies you can give them.

SYMBOLS

Activities have been coded for general age groups.

 means the activity is appropriate for younger children (approximately ages 3 to 8).

means the activity is appropriate for older children (approximately age 9 and older).

 means the activity is appropriate for all ages.

The abilities of children differ so much, these symbols are meant to be indications only.

REFERENCES

Throughout the book, we've referred you to other books which you may find in the library or in your local bookstore, just in case you want to know more. If you have a very good source, or a very good idea, write to us in care of the publisher, and we'll consider your information for our next revision! If we print your idea, we'll send you a free copy of the next edition.

GENERAL CONSIDERATIONS

- Be kind and patient. Children do not have the skills of adults. They often have short attention spans, and high energy (they get the wiggles in a hurry).
- If you have special chores that you must do, such as washing the car, or laundry, share your job with the kids.
- Be a good listener. Be a *non-judgmental* listener.
- Turn off the television set for the length of the

visit, or at least for most of it.

- Read to them. Choose a favorite book and read a chapter every day, such as *The Wizard of Oz*, or *Treasure Island*, or *The Secret Garden*, or *Robinson Crusoe*.

- Take time to teach your grandchildren about tools and how to use them. Teach the boys *and* the girls. Show them how to make repairs, if that is something you do. Teach them safety rules for using the tools.

- Take them with you when you go to the hardware store, the market, the bakery, and talk about what you see there.

- Find something new you'd like to learn about, such as another country, geography, the ocean, geology, or whatever, and invite the children to learn about it with you.

- Teach your grandchildren about the past. If you have old pictures, or keepsakes, tell the children about them. Memories to treasure!

Winning with Kids, T.A. Warschaw and V. Secunda, New York: Bantam, Doubleday, Dell, 1990

2. OUTDOOR ACTIVITIES AND DAY TRIPS

Enjoy the outdoors with your grandchildren. Kids love to be outside where they have lots of freedom to move (those old wiggles again!). Make sure they dress appropriately: plenty of clothes for cold weather, and if it's warm, take along a sweater in case it cools later in the day. Don't forget the sunblock. Even in the winter the ultraviolet rays can be intense.

Here are some of our favorite things to do outdoors, and some day-trips you can take as well.

FUN NEAR THE WATER

Are you near water? Even in the winter, an outing to the beach, lake, river or stream can be fun. In the warmer weather, bring lots of towels and a change of clothing. Make sure you have life vests for boating, and for fishing as well.

Water safety is no accident. Everyone, especially little ones, need to learn to respect the water without being fearful. Learning to swim is an important first step.

Swimming

 This one is loved by nearly everyone, and really good for you as well as your grandchildren. Teaching your grandkids how to swim may be one of your greatest contributions to their lives. Learning to swim is a must for boating, water skiing, surfing, paddle boarding, board sailing, skin diving and other popular water activities. Even fishing.

If you are not a good swimming teacher, swimming lessons are offered by the Red Cross, local YWCA, and other facilities in your community. It can be really enjoyable to be enrolled in a swimming program with your grandchildren.

Tide Pools

 At the beach, especially at low tide, tide pools are fascinating to children and adults alike. Check a tide table for the right time to go. This is another "teaching opportunity." Go to the library before your trip, or buy an inexpensive book at the bookstore, so that you can identify what you see in tide pools. Be sure to leave the creatures where they are, even though the kids are tempted to take home souvenirs.

> *The Audubon Society Book of Marine Wildlife*,
>   L. Lisse, New York: Abrams, 1980
> *Sea Anemonies*, U.E. Friese, Neptune City, J: TFH
>   Publications, 1972

Fishing

 A young, active, can't-sit-still-a-minute child can sit for hours with a fishing pole, trying to catch a fish. It's amazing. Kids will love digging worms up from your yard (a good way to get help turning the garden) or going with you to the local bait shop. Nothing is a bigger thrill than catching a wriggling fish on a little hook and trying to remove it, learning to clean it, and helping with the cooking for a scrumptious delight. Many grandmas and grandpas already love this activity, and will enjoy sharing it with their grandchildren.

If you need advice, the place to start is your local bait shop. The owner can advise you about inexpensive equipment, type of fish to go after, and locality. Fishing is the most fun when fish are caught!

If the fish aren't biting, have a good old-fashioned wiener roast followed by a marshmallow toasting next to an open fire. All great fun!

> *Field and Stream Magazine*, CBS Magazines, 1515
> Broadway, New York, NY 10036
> *The Complete Angler*, I. Walton, New York: P.F.
> Collier, 1961

Crayfishing

 While you're at the bait shop, ask for advice about catching crayfish, or crawdads. These delicious little fresh water shellfish can be caught in a commercially-made trap that you can purchase from your sporting goods department or store, or you can easily make one yourself out of wire screen. Use an open can of cat food for bait,

set it in quiet part of the stream, and pull it up an hour later, hopefully with a healthy catch. You can buy a dried mixture of herbs and spices especially prepared for a crayfish boil at the supermarket.

Boating

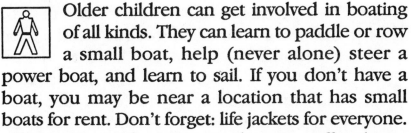 Older children can get involved in boating of all kinds. They can learn to paddle or row a small boat, help (never alone) steer a power boat, and learn to sail. If you don't have a boat, you may be near a location that has small boats for rent. Don't forget: life jackets for everyone.

Many cities and towns near the water offer classes in boating; so do colleges and universities. Call for information.

GO TAKE A HIKE

Nature walks and hikes are good exercise and learning experiences as well, and kids love exploring. In the big cities you will find informational walks and nature trails in the parks, and when you go out of town, there are even more opportunities. Let the children help plan the walk, or decide on the theme of the walk.

Be reasonable about the length of your walk, measuring the endurance of the children and yourself. Wear the proper shoes and clothing. Good shoes will prevent blisters and muscle soreness.

Know where you are going: be supplied with a very good map or take a compass if you are in unmapped territory. Teach the children how to use a compass. And *insist* that they stay with the group and not wander off alone. An enjoyable trip can end up a disaster if someone gets lost.

Set a theme for your walk.

It's for the Birds

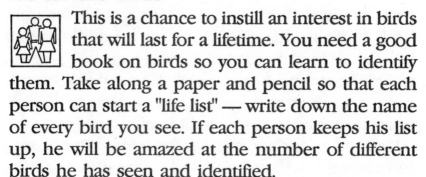 This is a chance to instill an interest in birds that will last for a lifetime. You need a good book on birds so you can learn to identify them. Take along a paper and pencil so that each person can start a "life list" — write down the name of every bird you see. If each person keeps his list up, he will be amazed at the number of different birds he has seen and identified.

If you have binoculars, take them along. Take a camera as well, and photograph the birds.

> *Birds of North America*, New York: Golden Press, 1983

Leaf Hike

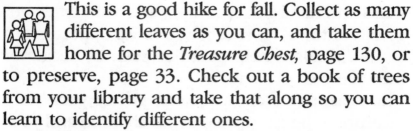 This is a good hike for fall. Collect as many different leaves as you can, and take them home for the *Treasure Chest*, page 130, or to preserve, page 33. Check out a book of trees from your library and take that along so you can learn to identify different ones.

> *Taylor's Guide to Trees*, Boston: Houghton Mifflin, 1988

Penny Hike

 This hike is good for small children in the city. Flip a penny at every corner, first deciding what heads and tails mean: "heads means go left; tails means straight ahead," etc. Talk about what you see: designs on buildings, plants in yards, trees, things in shop windows. For heaven sakes don't get lost; take along a street map. Even in your neighborhood, you might find great adventures you weren't aware of.

Wild Flowers and Plants Hike

 Armed with that ever-important library book (this time on wild flowers and plants), go on a wild-flower hike. Take along a paper and pencil and write down the plants you find. *Leave them where they are!* even if the children are tempted to pick. Save the beauty for the next group of hikers.

> *The Audubon Society Field Guide to North American Wild Flowers*, New York: Harry N. Abrams, 1985

Bug Box (or Jar)

You need a clear plastic box or a clear glass jar (the box is better, because it's not breakable), a magnifying glass and a good book on insects, and you're set for another outdoor adventure. Let the insect go after you've studied it and jotted down the name on your "lifetime list" of insects. Take a good book of insects along on your walk.

Audubon Society Book of Insects, Les Line, New York: Harry N. Abrams, 1983

Hiker's Picnic

 When you go on a hike, it's a good time to take along a picnic lunch. Of course no one person wants too much to carry, so it's best to make each person his own to carry, or have older children help you carry the lunch in backpacks. You can all plan and pack your lunch ahead, or if you're short on time, stop at the local deli on your way.

OTHER PICNICS

 The best picnics are those where you cook outdoors. Let the children help with the menu, the shopping, any food preparation done ahead of time and the packing up. If you're lucky enough to live near the sea shore, a clam bake or a fish fry are always a hit. But even hamburgers or hot dogs are fun to cook outdoors. Take along some toys, such as balls or frizbees. If you're going to a popular picnic site where you must make reservations, be sure to do so to avoid disappointment.

MUSEUMS AND MORE

 Visit museums, aquariums, gardens, planetariums and science buildings in your community. If you don't have these things where you live, plan on a trip to a nearby city where such facilities exist. You'll like these adventures as much as your grandchildren will, and everyone will add to their knowledge.

EVERYONE'S FAVORITE: THE ZOO

 Before you go, spend some time listening to and reading about animal habitats and behaviors. Some zoos offer guided tours or zoo keys to activate recordings that give information about the animals. Petting zoos which allow children to touch different animals are wonderful. Follow the feeding rules at the zoo, feeding only those animals you are allowed to feed, usually with food sold at the zoo. Animals can become very sick if you give them the wrong food.

The Complete Encyclopedia of the Animal World, D. M. Burn, ed., London: Octopus, 1980
The Book of Beasts, J. May, New York: King Publications, 1983

MEET YOU AT THE STATION

 Take a train trip with your grandchildren. This is especially fun for younger children, but everyone will enjoy it. Plan a one-day trip, returning home in the evening. Plan to go to a restaurant, or a theater, or a special event when you arrive at your destination. Make the trip a real adventure.

Call *AMTRACK*, 800-USA-RAIL, for train information.

THE BOOK TRIP

 Go regularly with your grandchildren to a bookstore and let each child pick out one paperback of his choice. He will build his library and his love for books. Go regularly to the library, as well, and let the children choose books to read during their visit with you.

VOLUNTEER

Take your grandchild to a home for the elderly, and let him read to one of the people there. Or take him to a "soup kitchen" for the homeless, and the two of you can serve people less fortunate than yourselves, or help with the dishes. Find other ways to volunteer your help; you will be teaching your grandchild a wonderful lesson in giving.

OUTDOOR SPORTS

Depending on your interests and the ages of your grandchildren, there are a tremendous number of outdoor sports that you can do together. Children may already by involved in team sports, but not in individual sports, and you may help them fill that void. Golf, tennis, jogging, down-hill and cross-country skiing, skating and cycling are wonderful exercise and do not have to be highly competitive. How long has it been since you've played croquet? Lawn bowling and horseshoes are not normally teen sports, but teens will enjoy playing with you.

MAKING AND FLYING KITES

Kites are a national pastime in several parts of the world, including the USA. Kites come in all kinds of shapes and sizes and are made of different materials, but mostly paper or cloth. The kites of the Orient have a particular significance. Traditionally, the Japanese fly kites on Boy's Day, one of their national holidays. The Chinese fly kites on the ninth day of the ninth month for good luck. Historians tell us that kite flying dates back to the 6th century BC in Greece.

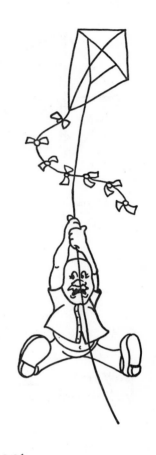

We all know about Benjamin Franklin's experiment flying a kite with a key on its tail, and that Alexander Graham Bell was a great kite flier. Kite flying had some military value in World War II, and many kites are flown for scientific purposes. But most people fly kites for sheer enjoyment.

The simplest kites are those that are classified as (1) flat kites, (2) bow kites, and (3) box kites.

Flat kites require tails. Bow and box kites do not. The kite tail can be made of lightweight rags tied together. The kite frame can be made from slats about ¼-inch by 1 inch wide and as long as you wish.

The flat kite will need two slats that can be formed

as a cross and tied together with string.

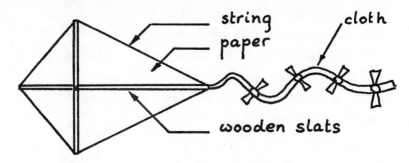

The bow kite also uses two slats but they must be made of material that will bend without breaking.

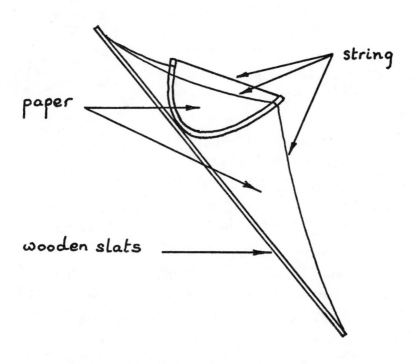

The box kite needs four slats for each of the corner uprights and two sets of cross members joined together in their centers, one set at the top of the box and the other at the bottom.

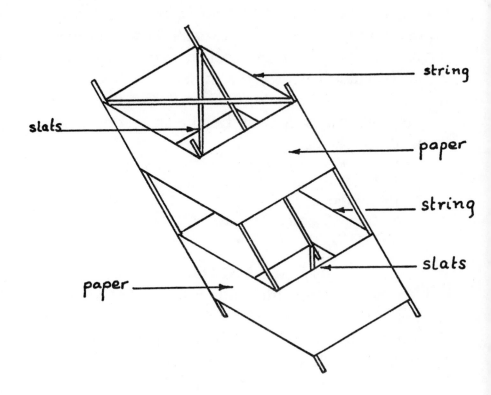

All three kites require string to connect the cross members and paper or lightweight fabric to cover the string.

Kites have also been made in the shape of dragons, fish and birds, some of the more popular kites today are really several kites flown as one, using dual controls. Flying kites of this type requires practice, strength, and skill. To be a good flier, the kite must be properly proportioned and balanced. The materials must be light, including the string.

The ideal wind velocity for most kite flying is between 8 and 20 miles per hour. Wire should never be used and kites should never be flown on rainy days, near power lines, and in heavily forested areas. Learning to crisscross the string (making figure eights) when winding the string in will make it easy to gather in or let out the kite as needed when flying the next time out.

The Complete Beginner's Guide to Making and Flying Kites, Edward Dolan, New York: Doubleday, 1977

Kite Lines Magazine, P.O. Box 466, Randallstown, MD. 21133

HOT AIR BALLOONS

What an exciting adventure! Hot air balloons are beautiful and very safe. Your grandchildren will love to float over the countryside with you. For information about balloon rides in your area, consult your yellow pages or write to:

Balloon Federation of America, P.O. Box 400, Indiavola, IA 50125

JUMP ROPE

You can have a lot of fun with rope and a little energy. Everyone can take turns being "turners" and "jumpers." Try using two ropes for "Double Dutch." It takes a little practice. Single jump ropes are good to have as well. Kids of all ages love to jump and do tricks with them.

BALANCE BEAM

 Young children, ages 3-6, can practice their balance and coordination by walking along a 2 x 4 on the lawn.

HOPSCOTCH

 This activity seems timeless, and enjoyable to every generation. Mark off a hopscotch with chalk on your sidewalk or driveway. How long has it been since you've played hopscotch? Join in!

FACTORY TOUR

 Arrange a tour of a local manufacturer to show your grandchildren how sugar is produced, or bannisters are made, or cheese is produced, or frying pans — whatever might be available for touring in your area. One grown-up we know says she remembers a tour of the cookie factory when she was a kid: "It was *so cool*!" Many manufacturers welcome tours, and will arrange a time for you by telephone. Your grandchildren will be educated, and so will you.

FIRE STATION

 Call ahead and make arrangements to tour the fire station with your grandchild.

Children are fascinated with firemen and their equipment, and you'll find the people at the station very cooperative and willing to teach children about what they do.

POLICE STATION

The people at the police station will also show children what they do, if they receive a call ahead of time. You may have a chance to see how calls are dispatched, inspect a police car, and talk to an officer about his job. Your grandchild will learn to understand and respect law enforcers.

VISIT A COURTROOM

Help your grandchild learn about the legal system: visit a courtroom and watch a trial in action. Call your local courthouse and get information about trials scheduled and hours. Read about court proceedings ahead of time, so you'll be able to name the "players": prosecuting attorney, defense attorney, judge, court reporter, bailiff, jury, defendent, witness.

VISIT A FARM

If your grandchildren are city-dwellers, a trip to a farm is a wonderful way to see domestic animals. We remember a trip with small children to a farm outside town, where there was a rope in the barn that you could swing on to land in a pile of hay, sheep with baby lambs, cows, geese, a pony to ride, chickens to feed and eggs in the henhouse. Call your county extension agent, who may know of a farm where you would be welcome. Find a lead in the classified ads in your newspaper, which list farms where you can pick fresh produce: the farmer may know of a farm with animals that welcomes visitors.

Take the kids berry-picking, or harvesting other foods from the farm; again, you'll find listings in the classified ads in your newspaper.

WHAT WE'VE LEFT OUT

Gliding, archery, horse-back riding, kayaking, canoeing, wind-surfing, climbing, racquet-ball — if we haven't hit the right ideas, the kids can add to the list!

3. GARDENING

Even if the grandkids are not going to be with you for an extended period of time, starting a garden with them is interesting, exciting and educational. Children delight in watching things grow into beautiful plants, some of which may be edible. Each time they visit they will explore what growth has taken place, and if the plants are edible, they will love eating from the garden. If you do not have a small place for a garden, you can make a container garden, or plant one or two pots.

START WITH EGG CARTONS

Don't throw away those egg cartons. They make wonderful containers for planting seeds. Wash them out after they are empty and fill them with potting soil. In early spring, plant your favorite flower or vegetable seeds in the cartons and watch them grow. The kids can pick out their own seeds and plant them—they can even take the carton home, if you wish.

Follow the instructions on the seed packet, or your nursery's directions. The key to starting plants from seed is to make sure the soil stays damp. Do not let it dry! When the seedlings develop their second leaf, it is time to thin them out to one plant per egg compartment. When the plants are larger, they can be transplanted to pots or to an outdoor garden.

You can also start seeds in empty milk or juice cartons, ice cream containers or old muffin tins.

INDOOR GARDENS MAY BE BEST

For city grandparents, container gardening may be the answer. Old vases or ceramic pieces, bowls or lined baskets make good containers, as well as ordinary flower pots. Usually they need to have a drain hole in the bottom for proper drainage.

Potting soil can be purchased at your local supermarket or at a nursery. Give the plant the proper amount of sunlight or shade. Some plants enjoy heat, and others like it cold. Consult your local nursery, an encyclopedia or a book on plants at the library for help. If you are planting from seed, planting instructions are usually on the outside of the seed packet. If you purchase seedlings from your nursery, ask for instructions when you make the purchase.

Caution your grandchildren not to over-water. Plants can be drowned.

How to Grow Healthy Houseplants, HP Books,
Los Angeles: Price, Stern and Sloan, 1979

Grapefruit Sprouts

 The next time you eat a grapefruit, save the seeds. Put them on a folded paper towel in a saucer, and keep the paper towel damp. Soon the grapefruit seeds will sprout. You can plant them in potting soil in a pot if you like, but this activity is primarily to watch the seeds sprout, which young children find fascinating.

Carrot Ferns

 Cut off the carrot top, leaving about 2 inches of the carrot, trim the leaves and put the carrot cut side down in a shallow dish or plastic container with water just covering the carrot. After it grows roots, plant it in soil. A pretty fern-like plant will grow. It likes water, so water often.

Potato Ivy

 If your potato has started growing eyes (white shoots), cut a piece of the potato off that includes one of the eyes. Place it in water so that half of the piece is above the water. To do this, stick three or four toothpicks around the piece of potato. Put it in a narrow glass jar or plastic container so that part of the potato is in water. (You can use a whole potato if you wish.) When the roots are well formed, the potato seedling or the potato can be planted in a pot. Potatoes make pretty vines, and can be placed in a hanging basket.

You can also do this with a sweet potato.

Garlic Shoots

 Garlic shoots are really simple to grow. Start with a few peeled garlic cloves and plant them directly into a pot filled with potting soil. The points of the clove should be facing up and barely covered with soil. It will need water, but try not to erode the soil around the clove. Plant it in a medium sized attractive container and keep it in the kitchen. The shoots will grow tall and the tops can be cut for use in cooking. Use garlic shoots just as you would use chives. The garlic shoot has a milder flavor than the garlic clove.

Herb Dish Garden

 Herb gardens are also great kitchen plants. They like sunlight, so put them on a window sill or near a window. They also like small containers with good drainage. Herb gardens are for sale and ready to grow at some grocery stores. Or start from seed or seedlings from your nursery.

Herbs are best to use when fresh, but if dried properly they can be stored and used later. When children get involved in growing a variety of herbs, they acquire valuable knowledge and taste for them.

Avocado Plant

 To start an avocado plant, put three toothpicks in the bottom third of the seed so it will rest partially in a glass or jar of water. You may wish to use a clear plastic cup to avoid breakage. When the seed is dry it may be hard to push in the toothpicks. Use round toothpicks; they are stronger and have sharper points.

Keep the seed indoors and monitor the water level so the bottom of the seed is in constant contact with the water. Shortly it will root and sprout. Plant it in a pot (if you live in a warm climate, plant it in the yard) and it will grow into a beautiful tree. Avocado trees get very large and need to be protected from the severe cold. If your plant is in the house, turn it often or it will bend toward the light.

Your tree will not bear fruit without a graft. Nontheless, your little seed will grow into a nice remembrance. All ages enjoy this project.

Nonedible Indoor Plants

Some indoor plants are easy to grow and do not take too much care, such as cactus, vines, succulents and ferns. Cactus gardens are especially easy to maintain and if kept in small pots will stay dwarfed. Some vines, such as ivy, Wandering Jew, piggy back and others, need to be cut back occasionally. Succulents are ideal for making terrariums in attractive containers. Ferns need light and water and should be thinned or transplanted when they grow to excessive size.

All of these plants can be grown in deep dishes or bowls, and they make very attractive gifts. Baskets can be planted with annuals; hanging baskets are attractive and easy to do. All of these indoor plants can be started by children of almost any age. They can be grown indoors in most locations.

Little Plants for Little Places, E. McDonald, New
York: Lippincott, 1974

Ortho's Complete Guide to Successful Houseplants,
S. Smith, ed., San Francisco: Chevron Chemical
Co., 1984

THE MAGIC OF BULBS

Most bulbs can be planted in containers. Tulips, daffodils, narcissus, crocus and hyacinths are some of the more popular bulbs that make pots of early spring blooms. Water hyacinths are the most interesting. For a nominal cost, a hyacinth glass can be purchased, and the kids can see the progress of the plant and its spectacular color as a result.

OUTDOOR GARDENS

If you do not already have a garden, developing the soil for a new garden could be a lot of hard work. We recommend you start with a small bed or plot that you and the kids can manage. Soil preparation is vital: consult your local nursery or look up the procedures in a book borrowed from the library. Kids are great help in digging and breaking down the soil.

The size of the garden will also depend on what you want to grow.

> *Complete Guide to Gardening,* Des Moine, IA: Better Homes and Gardens, 1979
> *How Does Your Garden Grow,* A. Wilson, Menlo Park, CA: A. Wilson Publishing Co., 1987

Vegetable Gardens

Vegetable gardens are always a pleasure, and the kids love to eat the crop at harvest time. Some vegetables like to live alone, and others don't mind company. Some grow fast, others slow, some mature in the spring and summer, and others in the fall and winter. A lot depends on the climatic conditions of your location. If you are new to gardening, ask for help in planning your garden. The people at your local nursery will be more than eager to help. Getting started correctly means success later on.

Home-Grown Jack-O-Lanterns

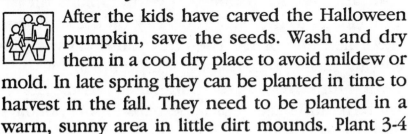 After the kids have carved the Halloween pumpkin, save the seeds. Wash and dry them in a cool dry place to avoid mildew or mold. In late spring they can be planted in time to harvest in the fall. They need to be planted in a warm, sunny area in little dirt mounds. Plant 3-4

seeds 1 inch deep in each mound, and space the mounds about 4 to 6 feet apart. Keep the mounds damp until the leaves start to form, and then irrigate around the mounds, trying to keep the leaves from soaking in water.

As the plants mature, they can be thinned to one strong plant for each mound. That plant will usually have the largest and healthiest fruit. Later, when fruit appears, keep one or two pumpkins on the vine closest to the plant root. Pick off the runts and deformed pumpkins. The ones you don't want for carving make great homemade pumpkin pies.

What fun! Growing the pumpkins, carving Jack-O-Lanterns and making pies, perhaps for the holidays. Save the seeds and roast them for a delicious, healthy snack. Take a picture of the kids with their harvested crop and later with their carved art. It should go in the family album, and will be a wonderful memory.

Flower Gardens

 When planting a garden for color, flowers can be a challenge. If you are already a gardener, you will have no problems, but if you are not, it might be wise to do a little research. Take a jaunt to the nearest nursery or library, ask questions and look in gardening books. Like vegetables, plants prefer certain climates and locations.

If you're lucky enough to have grandchildren who live nearby, they will be sure to see their efforts bloom. Those too far away, or who cannot visit at the right time, may have to settle for a snapshot. Cut flowers always make a hit when taken home to Mom, especially if their efforts helped to produce the results.

If you lack space, grow flowers in potted containers. A warm window in the sun is ideal for growing flowers as long as they are not being cooked with excessive heat. Start seeds in late spring and later transplant them into containers according to instructions on the seed packet.

HYDROPONIC GARDENING

Hydroponic gardening, or growing plants in nutrient-rich water rather than soil, has become very popular. Information about hydroponic gardening is available at your local nursery or garden supply shop, or at the library. The initial cost is paid back by the results.

Beginner's Guide to Hydroponics, James Douglas, New York: Pelham Books, 1972

POT-POURRI

How nice to open a drawer, closet, or enter a room that has been filled with a delightful scent. Pot-pourri is a mix of dried flower petals, herbs, spices and sometimes a scented oil. The mixture can be left in small open containers or it can be artfully tied into a small, square, porous cloth with a bow that can be stored in closets or drawers.

To make a dry pot-pourri, first check your garden. Rose petals are one of the sweetest and most important ingredients, but many flowers with a great deal of fragrance will work well. Some examples are carnations, honeysuckle, lilac, mock orange blossoms, lemon blossoms, pinks, freesias, jasmines; there are many, many more. Follow your nose.

The drying process should be done in a room without moisture to prevent mold. Remove the petals from the flowers and spread them on sheets of paper or trays in a single layer. Protect the petals from direct sun, which can be too severe, causing the scent to disappear. The drying process should take no longer than one week, depending on the weather. Some will dry more quickly than others. When they have dried, store them in air-tight containers. When the grandchildren arrive, bring out the containers and have the children help construct pot-pourri bags.

Many herbs and fragrant leaves can be added to the mixture of flowers. Some popular choices are lavender, rosemary, thyme, lemon verbena, bay, basil, mint, and sage. Cinnamon and nutmeg can be added to the mixture when combing flower petals and herbs. Dried orange and lemon peel also add fragrance. Scented oil can be purchased and added to a cotton ball for the base of the pot-pourri, or if desired the oil can be added directly to the dried flower and herb mixture. Use scented oil sparingly, only a drop at a time until you get the desired result, as it is very strong.

Pot-pourri make delightful little gifts that can be tied on packages or included inside a package to give and unexpected pleasure when the gift is opened. They can also be used as wedding favors instead of candy. The kids will love this project, because it is easy and pleasing.

A Book of Pot-Pourri, G. Duff, New York: Beauford Books, 1985

DRYING FLOWERS

 The ancient custom of preserving flowers is not difficult. There are three basic methods: treat the flowers chemically, dry by hanging, or preserve flowers by pressing.

Hang-Drying Flowers

Of the three, hang-drying is the easiest and works well with flowers that have seed heads, such as foxglove, iris, oats, barley, poppy and wild oregano.

Some plants dry beautifully in an upright position, such as pinks, garlic, lavender, Sweet William and goldenrod. Kept in an upright position, they retain their color.

Some flowers dry very well when left to stand in shallow water (about ½-inch in a pan) until the water evaporates. This method works very well with delphiniums and hydrangeas.

Some of the wild flowers dry better when kept flat on trays or on thick brown paper due to their weak stems.

Pressing Flowers

Flowers that press well are roses, honeysuckle and thyme. They must be totally dry when pressing them. Put the flowers between two sheets of waxed paper. Do not use newspaper, as the ink will enter the flower. Store the pressed flower inside a heavy book or under a stack of books.

Drying Flowers in Sand

Use fine, dry sand; sprinkle about 1 inch into a baking pan. Place the flower face up on the sand base, and sift 1 inch of sand over the flower, patting so that the flower will dry in shape. Bake at 200° for 20 minutes, and check to see if the flower is dry. Bake longer if necessary. Remove from the sand and place on paper to cool. Use a soft brush to clean the sand from the petals.

Preserving Flowers and Leaves with Chemicals

 Many of the colorful fall leaves will preserve best when they are chemically treated. A solution of 1 part glycerin and 2 parts water is ideal. Anti-freeze also works for plants like roses, daisies, daffodils, marigolds and carnations.

What To Do With Dried Flowers?

Dried flowers can be used in a number of ways: decorations for wall pictures, on greeting cards, and as ornamental arrangements for displays and centerpieces.

4. HOUSEHOLD CHORES

Everyday household chores can be laborious but are necessary. So that you and your grandchildren can have time together on more enjoyable pursuits, enlist their cooperation with the housekeeping. This way it is done quickly, and can even be fun. The secret is to teach the kids how to be organized, and how to go about their obligations.

Grandmothers and grandfathers are busy people these days, and a visit from the grandchildren can be a lot of work or a lot of fun. Kids won't mind doing chores if they feel it is important, and if they know it will make you happy. Compliments help make change; don't spare the praise and you will be rewarded.

All New Hints From Heloise: A Household Guide for the '90s, New York: Putnam, 1989

HOUSE RULES

 If everyone knows the rules from the beginning, there will be no misunderstandings. Develop house rules and make a game of it. Ask the children to contribute and you will find they will be more likely to follow the rules you have made together. You may want to write them down and post them in a handy place.

BED-MAKING

 Even small children can learn to make their own beds. If they are not perfect, compli-

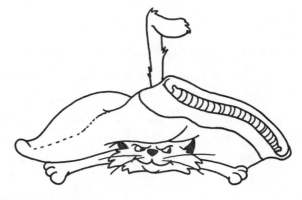

ment them anyway. Eventually they will do it as well as you.

HANG-EM UP!

Everyone can hang their own clothes. You may have to lower the clothes rod in a closet so little ones can reach. Grandpa can figure this out!

EMPTY DRAWERS

Find some empty drawers children can call their own, and show them how to store their folded clothes, even if they are only going to have a short stay. Give lots of compliments for keeping things in apple-pie order, and for saving time to do things that are more fun.

TOY BOXES AND STORAGE BINS

Have a box for storing the kids' toys and playthings, especially for the little ones. The box can be decorated with the child's name and should be stored where it can be found without your help. Get the kids in the habit each night before retiring of picking up playthings and putting the toy box away. Not just good organization, but a safety factor as well! Teach, "A place for everything, and everything in its place."

STEPPING STOOL

A small stepping stool is really handy for the little ones in the bathroom and in the kitchen. It does not have to be fancy, but it should be sturdy. It will help them when they brush their teeth and wash their hands and faces by themselves, and when they help out in the kitchen.

JOB JAR

 Write household tasks on small pieces of paper, fold them and put them in a job jar or basket. Everyone draws a paper out to find out his chore for that day, and the work gets done faster. Do it again for the next cleaning session so everybody has a change.

DUSTING, VACUUMING AND SWEEPING

 When everyone pitches in, these jobs can be done quickly in the morning and will eliminate a really big chore if periodically kept up. Little ones can use carpet sweepers and do some dusting. Big vacuum jobs can be done by older children.

FIRE ESCAPE ROUTE

Make a fire escape plan for every room in the house. Make a rough drawing of your floor plan with arrows showing the best way to leave; post it where everyone can see it. Hold a surprise fire drill occasionally for practice.

AFTER THE MEAL

When breakfast, lunch or dinner is over, everyone can help clean the table and get the dishes ready for washing. Many hands, no matter how small, make big jobs light. "Clear your own place, please!" is a good way to start.

IN THE BATHROOM

This is a potential disaster area! Teach your grandchildren to wipe the sinks after using, fold the towels and hang them back on the racks, give the mirrors and fixtures a quick wipe. Teach them where to find new rolls of toilet paper and boxes of tissues. "Leave everything the way you find it."

SHOPPING

Let the children clip coupons from the daily paper for the items you usually purchase (it's no bargain if the coupons entice you to spend *more* money!). Enlist their aid in preparing a shopping list. While you dictate, have them write down the items you will need. Ask them to categorize the list. For example, list all the fruit and veggies together, all the staple foods and paper goods together, etc. This will help when you enter the supermarket. Everyone can take part of the list and save time in shopping. Buying from a grocery list also helps them stay within a plan, a budget. Remember, don't shop when you are hungry!

OUTDOOR CHORES

Everyone can pitch in and do the necessary outdoor chores and get them over with. If you need to mow the lawn, rake grass or leaves, sweep walks or pull weeds, give each person part of the job, and it will be done much sooner. It's much more fun when a team works together.

THAT'S SHOE BUSINESS

A good rainy day project: assemble all the shoes in the house, and bring out the shoe-shine kit. Young children enjoy this, and everyone feels a sense of accomplishment when the shoes are all lined up and gleaming.

RECYCLING

Everyone can help sort glass from aluminum cans and bundle up newspapers. Take a trip to the recycling center when you're finished.

5. QUIET DIVERSIONS

When you've got too much to do, and grandkids too, they need an activity that can be done independently and quietly. The best activities keep the kids busy and learning, and give you time for the necessary things you have to accomplish. On rainy days it can be a real problem keeping kids entertained and out of trouble, especially when there is more than one.

Here are some ideas, and we bet you can come up with more.

PINT-SIZED MECHANIC

Many young children are fascinated for long periods of time with a screwdriver, a pair of pliers, and something to take apart. Buy an old clock, or a set of bathroom scales, or an old kitchen appliance at a garage sale. If you buy an electrical appliance, remove the cord for safety. Provide your grandchild with a tray or basket to put the pieces in. Children as young as four will enjoy this. We know one five-year-old who became so involved he took his old sewing machine to bed with him — slept with it next to the bed.

THE YOUNG OFFICE WORKER

For four-, five- and six-year olds (and older), a box of office supplies is great fun. Include transparent tape, paper clips, paper, pen or pencil, eraser, stapler, labels, and any other supplies that look fun.

CORN MEAL FUN

If you don't mind a little sweeping later, entertain a small one with a plastic dishpan full of cornmeal, and all kinds of measuring cups and spoons.

PATCH MATCH

 This is an excellent matching activity for small children. You need at least 20 different pairs of 2-inch squares of material. The child must find each square's mate by matching colors, textures and patterns.

BUTTON SORT — SORT OF

Do you have a collection of buttons in a box like most of us do? Have your young grandchild sort them into colors, sizes or materials, such as brass buttons, glass buttons, red buttons; or have him sort by size. Do you have any poker chips? Mix them all up and have your little one sort them into colors. Do you empty your pockets and coin purse into a jar? Let grandchildren sort coins; if they are able to, let them count the coins and put them into coin wrappers. Do all of your nails, screws, nuts and bolts end up in a pile? Let children sort them into containers for you.

MAGAZINE SEARCH

Put names of categories at the top of blank pieces of paper, one category per sheet: Furniture, Clothes, Fruit, Animals, Vegetables, People, Toys, etc. Provide the kids with old magazines, scissors (blunt scissors for the young ones) and paste or glue sticks. Tell them to find items for each category, cut them out and paste them on the right sheets.

THE FAMILY ALBUM

Do you have little piles of family pictures in boxes or drawers? Gather them together with an empty photo album and let a grandchild put them in. Be careful – if they don't know everyone in the picture, you might get some questions, and then the activity isn't really independent.

DRAW ME A . . .

Give your small grandchildren "art orders." They love to do this. "Draw me a man." "Draw me a house." "Draw me a monster."

CALLIGRAPHY

Calligraphy, the art of penmanship, has tremendous appeal and great value. It does not require a lot of expensive equipment and it is easy to do. Calligraphy books can be purchased at most book stores, and with a little effort, a youngster can become quite proficient. Calligraphy pens can be purchased at stationery stores, hobby shops and business supply stores. We suggest that you purchase a set, which includes different tips, ink cartridges and an instruction book. Some of the items that can be made with calligraphy are invitations, thank you notes, greeting cards, headings for stationery and addresses on envelopes.

You Can Learn Lettering and Calligraphy, G. Larother, Cincinnati: North Light Books, 1987
Woman's Day Book of Calligraphy, D. Droge, and Glander, J., New York: Simon and Schuster, 1980

SHAKESPEARE OR HEMINGWAY?

Creative writing has many facets, including short stories, plays, reports, novels, documentation and poetry. These are all great quiet activities. Get the kids to write about their experiences, vacations, hobbies, and almost anything else they can think of. Encourage them to be humorous; everyone enjoys reading funny stories, real or fictional. Rather than being immediately critical of writing skills and grammar, first enjoy and appreciate their stories. Get children to express their thoughts; later you can correct errors.

They should learn that every story has a beginning, a middle and an end. It is not necessary to go into detail about the various components of writing essays or reports. The message is the body of the story. It may or may not have a moral. A short story can be a mystery or have a surprise ending. Make writing fun. When children learn to love writing, school work will be easier.

Writing Poetry

Poems can be simple or complicated, they can rhyme or not rhyme, and the rhythm does not have to fulfill any set rule. The writer has tremendous liberty in their construction. The author can declare what he has written a poem whether it fits others' definitions of poetry or not! Read your grandchildren poetry that others have written for examples. Turn the children loose with a pencil and paper and encourage them to write poetry.

Miracles: Poems By Children of the English Speaking World, Richard Lewis, New York: Simon and Schuster, 1966

Rose, Where Did You Get That Red? Teaching Great Poetry to Children, K. Koch, New York: Random House, 1973

My Book of Children's Verses, Galley Books, New York: WH Smith, 1989

TYPING TOM OR TILLY

Playing with a typewriter has appeal for kids, and they should be encouraged to enjoy typing. For older children, pick up a "learning to type" book from a used book store, cover the keys with tape so they can't see the letters on the keys, and encourage them to work through the lessons.

If you have a computer, there are great typing programs that can teach kids how to use the keyboard and have fun doing it.

DO-IT YOURSELF COLORING BOOKS

 Coloring books are really enjoyable, especially for small children. Almost every youngster has a commercial coloring book. They are great teachers of color, shapes and coordination. Have your grandchildren make their own coloring books. Let them pick a theme and trace pictures from old magazines, newspapers or other printed articles like travel folders. This is a good project for the older kids who have younger brothers or sisters.

Keep pictures in a folder or a three-hole binder. Loose sheets of paper are easy to color or to use with tempera paints. Crayons are best, but colored pencils and inks can also be used. The pleasure of making their own book adds to the enjoyment of the finished product.

Vary the project by tacking a large sheet of paper on a wall and projecting a silhouette on the paper which is traced; it can be an object or the head of a family member, and it can be filled in by the young artist.

PAPER CUT-OUTS

 This quiet pursuit can be endlessly varied. Stand-up cut-outs can be made for dolls, cars, trains, trucks, boats — whole villages. Using old magazines, newspapers, greeting cards or any printed material that can be cut up, the kids can cut out figures and glue or paste them onto light cardboard. When the glue has dried, cut the cardboard out around the figure. The cardboard can come from old gift boxes or stiff packing material. Corrugated box materials are too hard to cut and not satisfactory. On the back of each cut-out, glue a cardboard stand which will allow the cut-out to stand erect. The stand should have a wide base to support the cut-out.

Children can create country scenes; street scenes with tall buildings, trees, cars; a zoo complete with animals; a car collection; anything old magazines and imagination can produce.

JIG SAW PUZZLES

If you have a place to leave a card table up for a few days, or if you have a table you will not be using, start a jig saw puzzle. They can be purchased at all levels of difficulty, and watch out! They can be habit-forming. You'll find members of your family sitting down to work on the puzzle between chores and other activities.

PAPER AIRPLANES

Paper airplane folding has been a quiet diversion ever since paper and kids were invented. It's a pursuit that every age loves, and you'd be surprised at some of the possible designs. This project can end in a contest, when you're ready to be a little less quiet.

The Ultimate Paper Airplane, Richard Kline, New York: Fireside Books, 1985

30 Planes for the Paper Pilot, Peter Vollheim, New York: Pocket Books, 1985

ORIGAMI

 Origami, or paper folding, has existed in Japan for centuries. This is somewhat like making airplanes, but more involved. Paper is not cut with a knife or scissors. Japanese paper figures are one of two types: they are used as decorations to be attached to gifts, or are used as table decorations. Paper can be folded into animals, flowers, humans or other objects.

Children learned geometry in German schools by folding paper into geometrical shapes in the 19th century, and the art of paper folding became very popular in Spain and South America during the early 1930s. Today many architects use paper folding in their construction of modern buildings.

A tip: visit your local printer, and ask him if he has paper scraps to give away. When he trims a job, often he has pieces of papers of many colors which he will discard. They are perfect for origami and other paper projects.

The Great Origami Book, Aytine and Scheele, New York: Sterling, 1987

Origami: A Step by Step Guide, N. Williams, New York: Hamlyn Co., 1974

Folded Paper Cutting

Using folded paper and a pair of scissors, make a series of duplicate figures, such as paper dolls. Make strings of figures to use for table or holiday decorations. Colored construction paper can be purchased at most stores which carry school supplies, but even the Sunday funnies can make a colorful design. Use white butcher paper for snowflakes, always a favorite.

SAND ART

Sand art in clear glass containers is interesting to do, and the results can be viewed for as long as you wish, discarded and done a new way. White sand can be colored with food coloring, and colored sands are easy to find at local craft shops and hobby shops. They are simply layered into a container and moved to create designs. You need a clear glass container such as a tall pitcher, or a vase, or even a jar with straight sides, a paintbrush, a spoon and a pointed tool. See *Arts, Crafts and Projects*, page 154, for more sand art.

Sand Art, Ellen Appel, New York: Crown, 1976

WATER TABLE

Do you have a place where water can splash a bit and not hurt the floor or surrounding area? Perhaps this activity could take place in the yard or on the porch or patio. Put a large basin of water on a table that your grandchild can reach easily, and provide objects that can be filled, that float, that soak up water — even paper boats. Wrap a large plastic apron around the child and let him experiment. Add soap suds and an egg beater, and let him use the bubbles to make bubble sculptures. You can also use the kitchen sink, providing a stool or chair to stand on. This activity is probably best for a single child, but is good for two if it doesn't deteriorate into a water fight!

APPLIANCE BOX HOUSE

Go to your local appliance store and get a carton that a stove, or refrigerator, or washer or drier has been shipped in, and take it home for an indoor house for your small grandchildren. Cut a door and windows, and let the children use crayons or paint for details. You will be surprised how many quiet hours they will spend in their house! They'll drag in their treasures, want lunch in there, and even nap-time.

6. INDOOR GAMES

Indoor games are good during the winter months and in the morning or evening when a little peace and quiet is necessary. Obviously the difficulty of the game should fit the ability level of the child. However, some very young children can learn simple games very quickly. And sharp youngsters can surprise you by understanding more complicated games. Don't be afraid to challenge them, but don't push them too far and make them discouraged.

There is a wealth of games for all ages in department stores and toy stores. Most board games list the appropriate age on the outside of the box. You should know that this is approximate and not always accurate. Games of chance are successful with younger children, because ability to play is not always a factor.

There are also numerous card games that you can play with your grandchildren.

We've listed some games here that we think are the best.

CARD GAMES

 There are a number of books in your public library that contain rules for card games for all ages. Some of our grandfather's favorites were cribbage, pinochle, bridge, big and little casino and solitaire games of all kinds.

Games such as *Pig, Fish,* or solitaire are good for young children. Sharp pre-teens and teenagers can learn bridge.

> *According to Hoyle*, Richard L. Frey,, New York: Fawcett Crest, 1970
> *Card Games for Kids*, J. Giannoni, New York: Golden Press, 1976

Cribbage

 Cribbage is a good game to teach children a little math. The game can be played by two, three, four or five players but is really fun when there are four players. The rules are simple and can be found in any encyclopedia. You need a deck of cards and a cribbage board. Buy one or make your own (see *Woodworking*, page 70).

Pinochle

Pinochle is another great game to teach children a bit about numbers. It requires a special card deck and a paper and pencil for scoring. Like cribbage, the rules can be found in an encyclopedia. Many pinochle decks come with instruction sheets. Difficult for children younger than seven because of the necessary knowledge of math.

Bridge

It may not have occurred to you to teach your grandchildren bridge, because it is sophisticated and requires knowledge of the game and memory. But by all means teach older teens the game, or if you have not played before but are interested, learn it together. It has universal appeal; there are national and international bridge championships played every year. There is usually a daily bridge column in the newspaper which is helpful to the beginner. Best source books are written by Hoyle or Goren, available in your local library.

> *Goren's New Bridge Complete*, Chas. Goren, New
> York: Doubleday, 1985

Hearts

 This is a terrific game that can be played by three to five players. Again, the rules are in your encyclopedia. You can keep score with your cribbage board.

Solitaire

 As the name implies, you can play solitaire alone, and there are many, many forms of the game. Solitaire games can be found in many books in the library, or in books at the bookstore or your local toy or hobby store. Games can be simple or complex, and can be played by all ages.

Card Tricks

 Some card tricks are simple enough for the youngest school age children to master, and even if they don't get it quite right, they think they are so clever you will be greatly entertained. Older children can become experts, and you may, too.

> *Self-Working Card Tricks*, K. Fulves, New York: Dover Publications, 1976

BOARD GAMES

 Checkers is one of the most popular board games, and can be played by young children. You can buy a checkers set or make your own board.

There are many commercial board games avail-

able at your local toy shop or in the toy department of your department store. Find a shelf in a bookcase or cupboard where you can store some games the children enjoy. Excellent early years board games include *Candyland* and *Chutes and Ladders*. *Sorry* is a good primary school-age game. Classics for older children include *Monopoly, Clue, Life, Yahtzee* and *Scrabble*. There are too many to list, and every year new ones appear. The advantage of board games is that a lot of players can get involved and they are great socializers — provided you don't get too competitive.

Chinese Checkers

 A variation on the checkers theme, Chinese checkers is played with marbles. Make sure the marbles aren't near tiny ones, to put in their mouths, nose, etc.

Chess

 This mind-stretcher is good for everyone, and can be very absorbing. If you don't know how to play, take time to learn to play it with your grandchildren. There are many books on this subject, and it can have life-long interest.

> *An Invitation to Chess*, Cherney, New York: Simon and Schuster, 1985
>
> *Chess in Ten Lessons*, L. Evans, New York: A.J. Barnes, 1974

Peg Board Games

 Peg board games, in which pins, nails or pegs are moved around a board with regularly placed holes, are wonderful quiet games that can be played by one person or more. See *Woodworking*, page 70, for directions for making a peg board.

Children can copy designs from paper, create designs and figures, or play a checkers-type game for two people. Start with a peg in each hole except one; any hole can be chosen to be vacant. The object of the game is to remove all the pegs except one by jumping them, checker-style. Jumps can be made in any direction, but once a peg has been jumped over, it must be removed.

Other peg board games can be found in children's game books.

EDUCATIONAL GAMES

Because something is labeled *educational* doesn't mean it isn't fun. Paper and pencil activities such as crossword puzzles are always challenging. Mazes are excellent for younger children. Wordquips and cryptograms are well liked by children. Wordsleuths are great vocabulary and spelling builders, but are also entertaining. Math squares and number squares along with number-connected drawings are found in the Sunday newspaper.

Dell Pencil Puzzles and Word Games, E. Rothstein, ed., New York: Bantam, Doubleday, Dell, 1990

Word Search Puzzles, Schuster, N. Dell, New York: Bantam, Doubleday, Dell, 1990

World's Best Crossword Puzzles, No. 5, Hayesville, OH: Landoll Inc., 1989

Best Travel Activity Book Ever, Chicago, IL: Rand McNally Inc., 1985

Construct a Crossword Puzzle

Crossword puzzles can be simple or very difficult, and so appeal to all ages. You can make puzzles for the children or they can make them for each other. Begin with a diagram, varying the shape and size depending on the age of the child, fit the words to the diagram, and develop the clues afterward. Build the puzzle around a theme. Pictures can be used for clues for young children, or they can construct the puzzle by using their own drawings or pictures cut out of magazines. Sports pictures from sports magazines, animal pictures from zoological magazines, or the Sunday comics are all good sources for pictures. Bring out the dictionary or a thesaurus for references sources.

Flash Cards

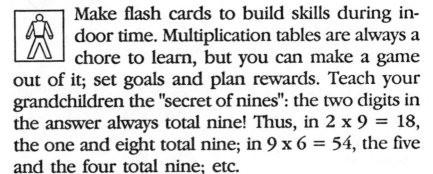

Make flash cards to build skills during indoor time. Multiplication tables are always a chore to learn, but you can make a game out of it; set goals and plan rewards. Teach your grandchildren the "secret of nines": the two digits in the answer always total nine! Thus, in 2 x 9 = 18, the one and eight total nine; in 9 x 6 = 54, the five and the four total nine; etc.

Cut flags from different nations from an old almanac to make flashcards.

Geography

Children to not seem to be learning geography in school, so add a little practice to your family activities. Photocopy the map of the United States or Canada in your telephone directory. Remove the names of states or provinces with white-out and photocopy again, making several copies. Let your grandchildren practice identifying the states or provinces. Do the same with maps of Europe and other places in the world.

COORDINATION GAMES

 All ages can play pick-up sticks, jacks, shuffleboard, and other coordination games. Don't be fooled! Young and old like to play such games. You'll find more in game books.

DARTS

 Find a place in your house, garage, basement or patio to hang a dart board. Invest in a reasonably good set of darts and join in with the older children. You may find that you really enjoy this indoor sport, which is becoming so popular in this country that there is regional and national championship competition.

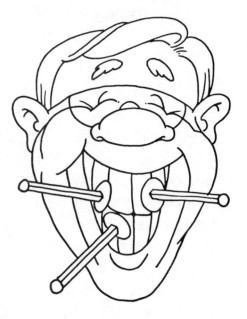

PING PONG

 Do you have space for a ping pong table? Or can you make a table that can be taken apart and stored when not in use? A large piece of plywood and several saw-horses will do the trick. This is another indoor sport that is fun for the grandchildren alone, or fun to play with a grandparent. And when the kids have gone home, you can challenge each other!

SCAVENGER AND TREASURE HUNTS

An indoor or outdoor game, a scavenger hunt is always a good time. Friends and neighbors can join in. Construct a list of clues for items to be recovered. Or hide small items around the house and give clues about their position. Or give players a list of facts to verify; they will have to use sources such as daily newspapers, magazines, dictionaries, encyclopedias, or even library references. The winning individual, or team that collects its list first has won the hunt.

Outdoor scavenger hunts should be not be too difficult; even the older children will give up if the challenge is too great.

Give prizes to everyone, but the biggest to the winners.

JOKES AND RIDDLES

Who thinks up jokes and riddles? Do they still tell elephant riddles? Children seem to know dozens of them, and think they're hilarious. Everyone will have a good time sharing jokes and guessing riddles. Appoint a judge to evaluate the jokes and award a silly prize. Or take turns stumping each other with riddles, giving time limits. This is a good way to spend a rainy afternoon away from the TV set.

SHAPE SEARCH

 This is a really good activity for little ones. Ask them to find these shapes in things in the house: triangles, squares, rectangles, circles and ovals. They might see a rectangle in a chair back, or a circle in a lamp, or a square in a pillow. Give lots of praise for good answers.

MYSTERY BAG

 Another good activity for little ones, this requires a paper sack and any household item that will fit in the bag. Ask the child to put his hand in the bag (without viewing the contents), feel the item and  guess what it is. If you have children of all ages, the older ones will enjoy playing this with their small siblings or cousins.

NAME THAT TUNE

 Tap or clap out the rhythm of a tune and ask the children to guess what the tune is. The winner taps out the next tune.

TRIVIA GAMES

 Homemade trivia games are mind-stretchers. Have children choose a topic and develop questions and answers from their own experience as well as available reference books. Then make sure they don't have the opportunity to answer their own questions. Try these topics: animals; sports; music; movie stars; hobbies; books and authors; geography; history; math; famous people.

MAGIC

You and your grandchildren might not be able to pull a live rabbit out of a hat, but other magical happenings are possible! In addition to books, you can buy magic kits and magic paraphernalia at your local toy store or hobby shop.

The Osborne Complete Book of Magic, Tulsa, OK: EDC Publishing, 1989

7. HOBBIES

Hobbies are usually considered to be pastimes that are of great interest, and often of lifetime duration. We suggest that if a particular hobby is something you feel possessive about, and not really willing to share, you shouldn't try. Some hobbies are not meant to be shared with young children, even though they may have a great interest in what you are doing. However, there is very little that cannot be shared if you are willing to do so. Listed in this chapter are some hobbies that can be scaled down to the ability of the kids.

Perhaps you will find a suggestion that will start you off on a new hobby, and you can explore it with grandchildren.

CERAMICS AND CLAY

 Ceramics and clay work has tremendous appeal to children. Supplies can be purchased at your local ceramic shop, where you will find a variety of "How To" books, magazines, greenware, glazes, information about different kinds of clay and tips on how to use clay. If you do not have a kiln at home, ceramic supply shops often have kilns, and will fire your pieces for you.

Potter's wheels are wonderful for older children, and local high schools, junior colleges and recreation centers may allow you to make arrangements to use their equipment, especially if you take a class in pottery.

Popular Ceramics Magazine, 3639 San Fernando Road, Glendale, CA 91204

Ceramics Magazine, Scott Advertising and Publishing Co., 30595 West 8 Mile Road, Livonia, MI 48152

Low Fire Ceramics, A New Direction in American Clay, S. Weschler, Syracuse, NY: Everson Museum of Art, 1986

Greenware

Greenware is a good place to start, and even kindergartners are not too young to join in. You can buy a wonderful assortment of items at your ceramics shop, including dishes, animals, dinosaurs, soldiers — just take your pick. Since greenware is just dried clay, it must be handled with care, but small children can do it.

Clay Cut-Outs

If you choose to use clay, at first treat it like cookie dough. Starting with white clay (solid pack), knead it into a workable consistency and use a rolling pin to roll it out to 1/8-inch thick sheets. Use a cookie cutter or a sharp knife to cut out different shapes. With this technique, you can make all kinds of interesting objects, such as Christmas ornaments, wall decorations, wind chimes, mobiles and package decorations for those special presents on birthdays, anniversaries and holidays. Cookie cutters can be purchased at your local kitchen shop or novelty shop, but sometimes it is fun to trace your own designs or cut-outs from magazines or newspapers. Do this while the clay is soft and pliable. In making your own designs, use a sharp knife and let the cut-out dry before trying to handle it. Drying may take a day or two, depending on the temperature of the air in the room where you are working. If you are making ornaments, wind chimes, or mobiles you will need to punch or drill holes before the clay gets too hard and brittle.

Wind Chimes

 When making wind chimes, vary the thickness of the clay to get an assortment of tones. This is a magnificent project and can be done by all ages with great success.

Liquid Clay and Molds

 Make your own greenware. Help the little ones pour slip (liquid clay) into molds, because the liquid in containers is heavy, and hard to lift. Results come out with a professional appearance. In glazing, care should be taken to use nontoxic glazes, especially on containers intended for food.

Clay Sculpting

 Sculpting with clay is always a pleasure and does not take a lot of talent. Odd-sized and shaped figures are truly pieces of art, and you should not look for perfection. Solid white or red clay works the best, although there are other clays that are acceptable. Decorating clay balls with fancy studs and pins for ornaments is easily done while the clay is still soft. Roll the balls into the size and shape you wish, and let them sit for a day or two before trying to decorate them.

WOODWORKING

There are a number of small woodcrafts that can be done with little or no special equipment. However, if woodworking is your hobby, or if you are interested in pursuing it, you probably have some tools in your possession already.

Basic Woodworking, Sunset Books, Menlo Park, CA: 1986

Woodworking Association of America, Box 706, Route 3, Plymouth, NH 03264, (615) 433-6804

Better Homes and Gardens Blue Ribbon Bazaar Crafts, G. Knox, ed., Des Moines, IA: Meredith Corp., 1987

Decorate a Box

A simple wood project that can be easily made is decorating the cover of a small box, perhaps a jewelry box or a box for small desk supplies. A cigar box works well for a base. First, remove all paper labels. Sand off paint. Stain the box inside and out. Glue a paper cut-out from an old greeting card, a paper decal or a drawing to the lid. Shellac or varnish the box's exterior and the decal will be preserved. You may wish to give it more than one coat. Some shellacs and varnishes will turn paper yellow, so make sure you use clear shellac or varnish.

Finally, line the inside of the box with felt, satin, or other attractive material.

Cribbage Board

 The game becomes more fun when Grandpa or Grandma helps the kids make their own cribbage board. This is not a difficult project. You need a small piece of wood, perhaps a piece of scrap lumber or the end of a wooden box. A hand drill is the safest, an electric drill works best, but a bench drill or drill press is even better.

The most difficult part of the cribbage board is making the pegs, so do those first. Cribbage boards for the kids are better with fatter pegs. Use a ¼-inch dowel cut into pieces about one inch long; make sure all pegs are the same size. Round off the ends with sandpaper, and sand the dowels until they are smooth. Make extra pegs, as they always seem to get lost.

Use a ¼-inch drill bit to make holes the same size as your pegs.

Peg Boards

 Peg boards for peg board games (see *Peg Board Games*, page 57) are made in a similar fashion to cribbage boards, but in different shapes, such as squares or triangles. When you have cut and sanded the dowel pegs, paint them different colors so colored patterns can be made. Make plenty of extra pegs so the kids can change designs.

Jig Saw Figures

An endless number of wooden figures can be cut out for book ends, lawn decorations, wall plaques, etc. Use outdoor plywood if the finished object will be in the weather. Otherwise, any plywood, pressed wood or masonite can be used. Trace the pattern on the wood from paper. Finish by sand-papering the object, staining and varnishing. Or you may want to paint it.

There are a number of inexpensive books on how to make movable toys, wind toys and other objects with a jig saw or scroll saw.

> *Making Wooden Toys That Move,* Alan and Gill Bridgewater,, New York: Sterling Publishing Co., 1986

Furniture Refinishing

This skill can be useful for life. Teenagers usually enjoy stripping furniture. Care must be taken to avoid ingesting toxic fumes either by inhaling or through the skin. Consult your local paint or hardware store for safe nontoxic paint or varnish removers that are easy to use and do not require a lot of time.

Start with small items of less value. Learning to repair dents and scars in wood is not difficult, and does not require a lot of expensive materials. There are kits available that make the job easy with professional-looking results. After some practice, the kids can move to a larger, perhaps more valuable piece of furniture.

Building Projects

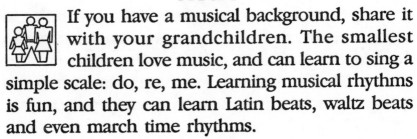

Many woodworking projects are long-term, but can be set aside and worked on again when your grandchild comes for the next visit. Such projects might include a scratching pole for a cat, a dog house, a bird house, a doll house, a small bench or stool, or other pieces of small furniture.

Tage Fried Teaches Woodworking: Furniture Making, T. Fried, Newton, CT: Tauton Press, 1985

MUSIC

If you have a musical background, share it with your grandchildren. The smallest children love music, and can learn to sing a simple scale: do, re, me. Learning musical rhythms is fun, and they can learn Latin beats, waltz beats and even march time rhythms.

Water Chimes

 Fill glasses with different levels of water and construct the scale for water chimes. It helps if you have a pitch pipe, a piano or other musical instrument to help you build the chimes. The children will have fun tapping the glasses with wooden or metal spoons to play simple melodies.

Musical Weed Reeds

 Musical reeds (oboe types) can be made using the stems from wild oat weeds. They can be found growing wild, perhaps in your backyard, in the late spring. Pull the stem from the plant to expose a hollow tube at its end. Cut off the end of the tube, about 2-3 inches. Pinch the tube about 1/4-inch from its end. The result is a small musical reed. Put the reed into your mouth and blow gently, and a musical tone will be produced. Vary the tones with the thickness and length of the reeds. Unlike the bamboo reed used with oboes, the weed reed has a very short life span, and cannot be saved for a long period of time.

Paper Tube Kazoos

 Save toilet tissue tubes, cut a few holes in them, and attach pieces of waxed paper to the bottoms of the tubes with rubber bands. They make lovely vibrating noises when you vocalize into them, similar to tissue-paper combs.

Dancing

 If dancing is your "thing," then this is right up your alley. Teach the kids your favorite dance steps, especially those old-timers that are forever popular: the waltz, samba, rumba, tango, jitterbug and even the real oldies like the Charleston and the Lindy Hop.

If you love square and folk dancing, here is your opportunity to practice your steps and teach the kids at the same time, especially basic calls and steps.

Aerobic dancing is very popular, and everyone will enjoy participating. Put your workout tapes on the video, or rent one from your local video shop, and have the kids join you for a workout. A perfect prescription for a good night's sleep!

PHOTOGRAPHY

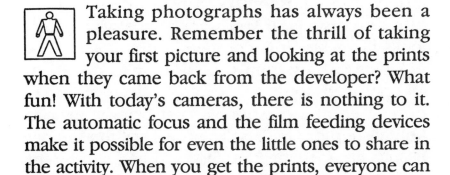 Taking photographs has always been a pleasure. Remember the thrill of taking your first picture and looking at the prints when they came back from the developer? What fun! With today's cameras, there is nothing to it. The automatic focus and the film feeding devices make it possible for even the little ones to share in the activity. When you get the prints, everyone can join in the fun of putting them in an album.

Older grandchildren can construct their own albums, decorate the cover, and make notations and labels alongside the pictures. Remind them to remember to put in the subjects' names and the dates!

Such an album is a great gift item.

> *Ten Secrets for Taking Dynamic Photographs,* HP
> Books, Los Angeles: Price, Stern and Sloan, 1988
> *Guide to 35MM Photography, 4th edition,* Kodak,
> Rochester, NY: Eastman Kodak Co., 1987
> *Electronic Flash,* L. Lefkowitz, Rochester, NY:
> Eastman Kodak Co. 1986
> *Close-up Photograph,* W. White, Rochester, NY:
> Eastman Kodak Co., 1984

ROCK HOUNDS

People who get bitten by "the rock hound bug" seem to have it in their systems forever. A good place for kids to start is by collecting specimens of different varieties of rocks and minerals. For a reasonable cost, you can invest in a rock tumbler and tumble rocks you have collected from nature walks, trips to the beach and other excursions. If you want to see what a rock looks like when it is polished, wet it.

Making jewelry from rocks is easy to do. Precut and polished stones and semiprecious gems can be purchased at a reasonable cost from your local hobby shop or lapidary. They also sell the settings. Results are extremely professional and small items such as pins, cuff links, tie tacks, bracelets, necklaces, stick pins and rings can all be made using rocks and stones for gems. The settings, mountings and chains can all be purchased from your lapidary.

Simon and Schuster's Guide to Rocks and Minerals, New York: Simon and Schuster, 1976
Rock Hunter's Range Guide, J.E. Ransom, New York: Harper Row, 1962
Making Your Own Gemstone Jewelry, Blue Ridge Summit, PA: Tab Books, 1988

MODELS

Model building is an absorbing hobby for many people of all ages: ships, airplanes, cars and more. Have you been to a hobby shop recently? You will be fascinated at the assortment of models available. Many models are inexpensive; model trains are the costliest, and you can construct scale models of buildings and scenery in addition to trains. You can even build your own engine, paint it and put the motor in it!

A model plane with a radio control unit can be made for less than $200, and will give hours of fun outdoors after completion.

Model Railroader Magazine or *Fine Scale Modeler Magazine*, both from Kalmbach Publishing Co., 21027 Crossroads Circle, P.O. Box 16122, Waukesha, WI 53187

SEWING

Sewing simple items such as aprons, place mats, tablecloths and towels does not require a lot of special skill. If sewing is something you often do yourself, it's an excellent interest to pass to grandchildren — with a really important pay-off, for if they become skilled, they can save a great deal of money.

Place Mats

Here's a "sewing" project that requires no sewing: making place mats with a pulled string fringe. Take a trip to the fabric store to purchase the proper material. Buy the material so that a set of place mats includes several different colors, if you prefer. Cut the mats to size, planning for fringe of approximately ½-inch. (Measure one of your place mats, or measure place mats in a store to get the size you prefer.) Then pull the threads, one at a time, from each side of each mat until the fringe is the right length.

You can make matching napkins with squares of material. This project makes a beautiful gift.

Pin Cushions

Make a pin cushion in the same manner that you made stuffed animals and dolls, but stuff the cushion with a substance that will grip the pins and needles. Foam rubber works, as does horsehair and kapok. Old styrofoam Christmas ornaments can be recovered with scraps of material and made into pin cushions; round ones should be flattened on one side with a sharp knife before covering.

Dolls From Rags

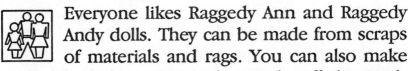
Everyone likes Raggedy Ann and Raggedy Andy dolls. They can be made from scraps of materials and rags. You can also make stuffed animals, or repair damaged stuffed animals using rags and left-over materials. Copy a picture of a horse on paper. Cut out two copies of the horse from a folded piece of material. Sew up the edge, leaving a small opening, and turn the animal inside out. Stuff it with scraps and sew the opening shut. Viola! A stuffed animal! Use buttons, scraps and yarn for details.

The children can draw their own animals for more imaginative toys. If they need to, they can trace a picture from a magazine or newspaper. Coloring books are also good sources for patterns. Old photographs can be used as well.

Scrap Bag

 Keep a bag or a box of scraps of material for your grandchild. Include felts, leather scraps, gold lamé, satin and other "fancy" fabrics if you can. Let your grandchild construct doll clothes with a needle and thread; help with simple patterns.

Hats for dolls can be made using felt. Cut a piece of felt into a circle large enough to fit over a mold (a small bowl for a large doll, a bottle cap for a small one) with enough left over to make a brim. Soak the felt in a mixture of white glue that has been thinned with a little bit of water. Center the felt on the mold and form it carefully with your fingers, stretching the wet felt to fit the mold exactly; spread the edges out to make a brim. Let the felt dry completely, and then remove from the mold. Your hat will look very professional. Trim it with ribbons if you like.

KNITTING AND CROCHETING

First-graders can learn to knit simple squares, and if you are a knitter, why not start your grand-child on a simple project? Following World War II, school children knitted squares to make blankets for the "Bundles for Britain" effort. A few squares, sewn together, can make a blanket for a doll. Or one long knitting project can produce a scarf.

Simple crocheting can also be done by primary age children, if they are interested and you are willing to teach.

COLLECTIONS

Collections have life-long value. The most notable is stamp collecting. This popular hobby is enjoyed worldwide by people of all ages. It is easy to get started. Albums can be purchased at the post office, hobby shop, toy store and most department stores. Most libraries have instructional books, and stamp clubs can be contacted through your phone book or local newspaper. Stamp clubs readily invite junior members and they are the best source for getting the kids started.

Other ideas for collectables: coins, matchbook covers, salt and pepper shakers, toy soldiers, toy airplanes, toy automobiles, tin toys, printed napkins, song sheets, autographs, sports cards such as baseball cards, posters, handbills, business cards, political campaign buttons, other election materials, theater, concert and sports programs, ticket stubs, samples of different kinds of rocks and minerals.

We know you can think of others. Help your grandchildren get started, and keep them interested.

The Stamp Atlas, W. Wellsted, New York: File
   Publications, 1986
Collector's Index, P. Turner, Westwood, MA: F.W.
   Faxon, 1980
Coin Collectors Handbook, F. Reinfeld, Garden City,
   NY: Doubleday, 1976
1990 Coin World, New York: New American Library,
   1989
Coinage Magazine, Miller Magazines, 266 East Main
   Street, Ventura, CA 93003
Beginner's Guide to Stamp Collecting, Ted Schwarz,
   New York: Prentice Hall, 1987
Coin World Magazine, P.O. Box 150, Sidney, OH
   45365
Linn's Stamp News, P.O. Box 150, Sidney, OH 45365

HAM RADIO

Would you like an exciting hobby that will fascinate your grandchildren and yourself? One that allows you to talk to bricklayers, kings, garbage collectors and senators from one mile to thousands of miles away? For about as much money as you would invest in a video recorder and camera, you can be a ham radio operator. Many communities have outlets that sell second-hand equipment. You need to pass a test to obtain a license. Get information about clubs in your area from your local FCC office, or from Civil Defense. Or write to:

American Radio Relay League, 225 Main St.,
   Newington, CT 06111
How To Be A Ham, W. Edmund Hood, Blue Ridge
   Summit, PA: Tab Books, 1986

HOME AQUARIUMS

Home aquariums can be purchased at your local aquarium store or novelty store. Ask for instructions, and costs for plants for the tank, food and other supplies. There are several different kinds of tanks, and their uses vary with the type of fish they will contain. Standing water tanks do not need special aeration devices, but they must be cleaned more often than those that do. Air pumps will keep the necessary supply of oxygen in the tank for the fish to survive.

Some fish live well in fresh water, while others need salt water. Some need very little care, and others are delicate and need special care. Most of the fish kept in home aquariums are labeled *tropical* because a vast number of them come from the tropical areas of the world.

Home aquariums are entertaining, and the kids will watch the fish by the hour. Find out more from your local supplier.

> *Freshwater and Marine Aquarium Magazine*, P.O. Box 487, Sierra Madre, CA 91024
>
> *Setting Up An Aquarium*, J. Kelly, Neptune City, J.J.:TFH Publications, 1987
>
> *Marine Aquarist's Manuel*, Morris Plains, NJ: Tetra Press, 1983

8. COOKING WITH THE GRANDKIDS

Cooking is always fun for your grandchildren. This is a time the kids will never forget, no matter how complicated the process. Prepare head of time, with an apron that will fit, a stool to sit on, or a small bench to stand on. Getting the food ready will take awhile longer, but the results will be well worth the effort.

It is wise to teach children a few safety rules, such as how to use a knife and other kitchen implements. With little ones, it is important to supervise use of knives, cutting and shaping tools, mixers and blenders, toasters, waffle irons, cooking surfaces and oven.

Some recipes will require your help. Because the kitchen can get messy, give kids some freedom to experiment, but also require them to clean up afterwards. Keep cleaning tools and implements where they are accessible, but keep toxic cleansers, lye, strong acids and other caustic materials out of harm's way. To avoid worry about breakage, keep all fragile dishes and glasses where they cannot be reached, or make them out-of-bounds.

BREAKFAST IS EASY AND FUN

Breakfast is a great place to start, because of the variety of possible foods that can be prepared with little or no difficulty. And since it's a meal that is sometimes neglected, doing something a little special will encourage you to have a healthy start.

Try these ideas:

- Eat outdoors.
- Be artistic: cook pancakes in animal shapes; slice fruit into decorative arrangements; carve melons into fruit baskets; slice toast into triangles; use cookie cutters to make toast shapes; spread toast with cream cheese or peanut butter and decorate with faces made from raisins, pieces of dried fruit and coconut.
- Use food coloring for special effects.
- Display food attractively on plates and serving platters.
- Serve Grandma and Grandpa in bed (are you ready for this?).

- Use the blender for mixing fruit juices. Add ice and blend on high. Juices will never taste better. Mix orange and pineapple or orange and cranberry juices. Mix other combinations for color and taste.
- Serve hot or cold cereals with colored sugar crystals and fruit.
- Buy glasses, mugs, or cups with your grandchildren's names on them; buy some for yourself, too.
- Add music to make breakfast an even happier time.

FOOD IDEAS FOR BREAKFAST

Kids love variety and something different than they normally get at home. Add these suggestions to your favorite recipes:

Decorated Bacon and Eggs

 Place two or three pieces of bacon on top of a piece of toast to simulate a raft and then place an egg (any style) on top to be the passenger. Give it a special name, like Kon Tiki, Eggciting Raft or Tom Sawyer's Raft.

Herbed Eggs

 Scramble or baste in olive oil with fresh garlic cloves and your favorite herbs.

Fancy Cereal

 Decorate the dry cereal bowl with fresh, canned or frozen fruit around the edge. Or use dried fruit pieces.

Volcano Cereal

 Make a crater in the top of hot cereal for the milk and call it your favorite volcano (Kilauea, Mt. Etna, Mt. St. Helens); float a red cherry in the milk for a special effect.

Fancy Faces Cereal

 Decorate hot cereal with faces made from pieces of fresh or dried fruit, nuts and coconut.

Multi-Colored Juice

 Pour juice into glasses in layers — first orange, then cranberry, etc. Grandpas have fun with this one.

Pigs in a Blanket

 This is a good one for teens to make. Use a variety of sausages. Wrap cooked pancakes around cooked sausages, cover with powdered sugar, syrup or your favorite jam or jelly. Yum! Yum!

Butter Molds

 Make butter or margarine balls, shells, or other shapes with molds (available in cooking shops). Leftovers can be used for other meals. Make a lot and store them for later use.

Breakfast Cones

 Fill ice cream cones with yogurt or applesauce and sprinkle with granola.

Continental Breakfast

 Always a hit with the kids, a continental breakfast gives every person a chance to choose his own breakfast from an assortment. Serve fruits, fresh in season, canned or frozen; juices; cereals; sweet rolls or other breads, jams and jelly; milk; a variety of breakfast meats such as bacon, Canadian bacon, linguisa, bangers, pork sausages, chorizo, Italian sausage, bratwurst or knockwurst; fish such as pickled herring, sardines, smoked salmon or tuna; an assortment of cheese; coffee and tea.

Breakfast Sandwiches

 Make sandwiches out of waffles, using eggs, breakfast meats or fruit spreads and peanut butter as fillings.

Fruit Kabobs

 Put chunks of fruit on wooden skewers and serve them on a platter. Include pieces of banana, apple, orange, grapefruit, kiwi, pear or other fruits in season.

Toast Delights

 Toast can be made of many different kinds of bread for variety. Some breads are better toasted in the oven or in a toaster oven. Once browned they can be spread with butter or margarine and topped with sugars, preserves, nut butters or another favorite topping. (Nutella, Italian hazelnut chocolate syrup, is a real delight — find it at your deli.) Mix your favorite spice, cinnamon or nutmeg with sugar to add a different taste. Go international with bread. Try bagels, biscuits, corn bread, French bread, Irish soda bread, matzoth, tortillas, Panatone (Italian), Portuguese sweet bread, Scotch bannocks or Swedish crackerbread.

Scrambled Eggs Fajitas

 Put all the fillings in bowls and let everyone make their own breakfast. Set out tortillas warmed in the oven in foil, scrambled eggs, chopped green chiles, chopped black olives, chopped green onions, salsa, shredded cheese (cheddar, Jack or your choice) and chopped fresh tomato. Serve with vegetable juice or tomato juice poured over ice cubes.

LET'S EAT LUNCH

Lunch is a time for a lighter menu, with salads and sandwiches heading the list for popularity. Nevertheless, lunch can be great fun for you and your grandchildren. Try some of our ideas:

Lunch Kabobs

 Put squares of cheese, meat cubes, chunks of vegetables, olives and pickles on wooden skewers.

English Muffin Pizza

 Use English muffin halves as the base for individual pizzas and top with pizza sauce, cheese, Italian lunch meats, onions, olives, mushrooms, slices of green bell pepper, and other favorites. Place under the broiler or in a toaster oven to complete; serve warm. Each miniature pizza can be different, made to suit each person's wishes. This idea requires little preparation and leaves very little mess to clean up. Little ones need some help.

Open-Faced Sandwiches

Be creative with cookie cutters, or cut the bread into shapes of your own, such as triangles, circles or stars. Encourage children to be inventive. They can make boats, airplanes, autos, or other shapes and decorate with garnishes.

For toppings, use standard luncheon deli-meats and cheeses, or make a variety of fillings and spreads using a cream cheese or cottage cheese base. Add to the base chopped eggs; chopped olives; cooked, crumbled bacon; chopped green onion tops; grated carrots; left-over diced chicken, ham, turkey or beef; minced pickles; minced pimiento; chopped cucumber; chopped radishes; or any combination. You will think of other ingredients!

Decorate open-faced sandwiches with lettuce, parsley, sliced onion, pimiento, or any other item that will add color and make the product attractive. Sometimes a sprinkle of a spice or an array of nuts on top can embellish the appearance and taste.

Nothing pleases the kids more than compliments for their preparation and presentation of a tasty dish.

Long Baguette Sandwiches

Easy to make, delicious to eat, and popular with kids. You may have to slice the long baguette or roll in half for the little ones, and maybe into sections before eating. Provide mayonnaise, butter, cream cheese, or your favorite spread for one side of the entire loaf, and mustard or whatever appeals to you on the other side. Have children layer meats, cheeses, tomato slices, lettuce and pickle slices to cover the entire half-loaf. Cover with the other half and slice off pieces for everyone.

Pinwheel Sandwiches

These are more complicated, but can be lots of fun to make. Use a whole loaf of unsliced bread, and trim off crusts on all four sides. (Save the crusts for croutons or garlic toast.) Slice the bread into ¼-inch slices lengthwise. Top bread with your favorite fillings; soft fillings work best, but shredded meat can be used. When the bread is covered to your taste, start on one side and roll it up like you would a jelly roll, not too tight, but firm enough to make the bread remain in a roll. Wrap with plastic wrap and refrigerate. When ready to eat, cut diagonal slices and place on trays. Garnish with olives, pickles, radishes, cucumber, lettuce or any of your favorites. Cut with a serrated knife to avoid crushing the bread roll.

Fresh Fruit Animals

A good way to get the kids to eat fruit for dessert rather than sweets is to make fresh fruit or canned fruit animals or other designs (canned salad fruit contains a variety of fruits). Here are some Grandma used to help us with:

- Make a four-legged animal (horse, cow, dog, deer, elephant) using an apple, pear or orange half for the body. Make the head from a smaller piece of fruit. Make the legs from pieces of banana. The tail can be made from a date or a slice of apple, orange or pear.
- Make a wheel of dried fruit. The hub can be a dried apricot, the spokes can be raisins, and the tires can be dates.
- Make trees from grapes, nuts and dried fruit. The trunk can be a series of pecan nuts or almonds, the branches can be grapes, and the blossoms can be pieces of dried fruit, apricots, apples, pears or prunes.
- Make a fruit train. Use different fruit for box cars. Wheels can be grapes or cherries, and railroad tracks can be raisins or nuts. Cut larger fruit (apples, bananas, pears oranges, peaches, nectarines and apricots) into shapes for cars and locomotive.

DINNER IS A SPECIAL TIME

Dinner with Grandma and Grandpa is always a special time, and more so when the kids get to help. When kids are included in preparing the food, you will find they are usually good eaters, and even more so if they have a hand in selecting the menu and planning what to eat.

Some kitchen chores can be fun, such as peeling potatoes and carrots, or other vegetable preparation. One of the things kids can do is cut the vegetables into attractive shapes. This can be done with little or no supervision for older children but some of the younger ones may need help, or they may need to do another chore than doesn't require a knife. Get out the cutting board and sit around the kitchen table; have fun being inventive and artistic. Try these ideas:

Princess Anna Potatoes

Peel and slice a potato into ½-1-inch slices, coat with butter or margarine, wrap in foil and bake in a 375° oven for 30 to 45 minutes, depending on the amount of potato. Wrap each person's portion separately, which will allow you to judge how much to give to each child. Serve in foil wrappers on the dinner plates. Each child can unwrap his own for the potato surprise inside. You can vary this by using a cookie cutter on the potato slices, or by cutting various shapes by hand. Place in water to prevent cut slices of potato from turning brown. Wrap scraps in foil to be baked for seconds or leftovers.

Shoestring Veggies

Using a French fry potato cutter, cut carrots, squash, and other veggies into long skinny strips prior to cooking. After they have been cooked, they can be arranged on a plate as a sunburst or flower. Use the fat ends as the center of the design. They can be steamed, microwaved or even deep-fried. Encourage the kids to be artistic — it will help them eat their vegetables.

Veggie Balls

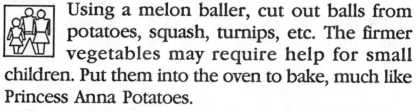

Using a melon baller, cut out balls from potatoes, squash, turnips, etc. The firmer vegetables may require help for small children. Put them into the oven to bake, much like Princess Anna Potatoes.

The veggie balls can also be steamed, boiled, or cooked in any manner you would cook potatoes. When steamed or boiled, they can be served with butter and parsley, or with hollandaise sauce. Or mix them into your favorite stew. Thread them on skewers and barbecue them as part of shish kabobs. Dip them into batter and cook them tempura style. One thing is sure: the kids will eat their vegetables and have fun preparing them.

Ants on a Log

Prepare celery stalks, especially the tender inner stalks, and cut into pieces about 2-3 inches long. You can leave the tops of the celery on the stalks. Spread on peanut butter or your favorite cheese spread. Put a row of raisins or nuts on the peanut butter or cheese spread.

Vegetable Decorations

After potatoes have been mashed, use a cake decorator to make decorative designs on the serving platter or on each dinner plate. For a different, delightful flavor, add other mashed vegetables to potatoes, such as parsnips or turnips.

Raw Vegetable Art

Use a sharp knife or a potato peeler to cut celery stalks, carrots, jicama and other root vegetables into long thin strips. Mushroom caps, half radishes, olives, cherry tomatoes, cauliflower corms and broccoli spears can all be used to make beautiful arrangements on a relish tray. Place around your favorite veggie dip.

Potato or Taro Baskets

Shred raw potatoes or taro root and quickly mix with a beaten egg, one tablespoon of flour, a pinch of salt, and a tablespoon of oil. Grease a muffin tin and shape the mixture with your fingers and a tablespoon to line each muffin cup. Use just enough mixture to cover the sides and bottom. Bake in a 400° oven until lightly browned. When done, remove from the oven, fill with colorful cooked vegetables (peas, carrots, green beans) and serve.

DESSERTS TO REMEMBER

Making desserts is often the most enjoyable task

you can share with grandchildren. Start a collection of recipes in your own handwriting for each child. They will be lifelong keepsakes. We still have some of Grandma's recipes, written by her, and they are among our favorite readings and doings.

Fortune Tea Cookies

This is a really fun cookie recipe which everyone can pitch in and help with. Allow 1½ to 2 hours for this project. The activity that leads up to the cookies is the first part of the fun. Everyone must write a "fortune" on a small piece of freezer wrap that is cut ½ inch x 2 inches. Children can write proverbs, sayings, predictions, and other words of wisdom. Here is the recipe:

> 3 egg whites
> ¾ cup sugar
> ⅛ tsp. salt
> ½ cup butter or margarine, melted
> ¼ tsp. vanilla
> 1 cup sifted flour
> 1 tbs. instant tea
> 2 tbs. water
> paper fortunes

In a medium bowl, combine egg whites, sugar and salt. Stir in, one at a time, butter, vanilla, flour, tea and water. Chill in the refrigerator at least 20 minutes. On a greased baking sheet, drop 1 slightly rounded teaspoon of dough for each cookie, keeping them about 4 inches apart. Spread the dough very thin with the back of a spoon so that it is about 3 inches in diameter. Bake 5 minutes at 350° or until edges turn light brown.

Remove immediately to a wire rack. Cookies

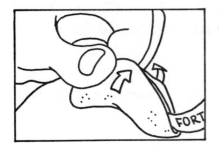 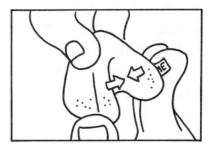

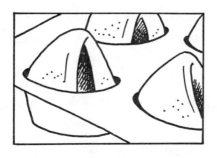

should be paper-thin. Quickly place a paper fortune in the center of the cookie. Fold the cookie in half to form a half moon. Grasp the rounded edges of the moon between the thumb and forefinger of one hand. Place the forefinger of the other hand at the center of the folded edge. Push in, making sure the solid sides of the cookie puff out. Keep the forefinger in place while bringing the edges of the fold downward around the forefinger. Place each cookie in a small muffin tin. Open edges up until the cookie cools completely. Store in an air-tight container.

Seasonal Desserts

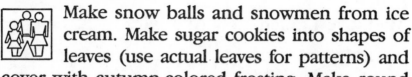

Make snow balls and snowmen from ice cream. Make sugar cookies into shapes of leaves (use actual leaves for patterns) and cover with autumn-colored frosting. Make round yellow summer suns, and lamb cookies for spring. Cookie cutters for Halloween, Thanksgiving, Easter and Christmas are all available at your local kitchen shop.

Cake Decorating

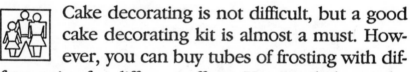

Cake decorating is not difficult, but a good cake decorating kit is almost a must. However, you can buy tubes of frosting with different tips for different effects. You can bake a cake and decorate it for almost every occasion without too much effort.

Ask the kids to draw a picture on paper first, about the same size as the cake, and then copy it on the cake. Use a simple sheet cake. Practice on waxed paper or the shiny side of freezer wrap. Practice makes perfect, and is "finger-licking" good.

Baker's Buttercream Frosting

1½ cups margarine or shortening
½ cup sweet butter
1 lb. confectioner's sugar

1 tsp. vanilla
pinch salt
4 egg whites, room temperature

In a mixer bowl, mix at low speed margarine, butter, sugar, vanilla and salt until smooth. Add one egg white at a time and beat well at high speed after each addition.

Separate frosting into small bowls. Add food coloring and flavoring to each batch. Fill the decorating tube with frosting and go for it.

If your grandchildren really enjoy cake decorating, and you find that you do, too, there are books available in your kitchen shop or library that will give you special information about flower-making and other special effects.

> *Cake Decorating*, Jane Suthering, Secaucus, NJ: Chartwell Books, 1984
>
> *Cakes and Cake Decoration*, Denise Jarrett-Macauley, New York: Exeter Books, 1985

Cake Decorating With Plastic Figures

 Inexpensive figures can be purchased from a toy or novelty store, such as toy baseball players, automobiles, airplanes and the like. These can save time and usually make a professional looking decorating job.

Cake Decorating With Candy

 Candy animals, Santa Clauses and even flowers can be purchased at a candy store. Chocolate flowers are quite delicious.

Sundaes

 Make sundaes with multiple flavored ice creams or sherbets served in stemware. Each person can choose his own toppings. Chop some nuts to sprinkle over all, and add maraschino cherries at the top. Or add banana halves to make banana splits in bowls.

POPCORN SNACKS

One of our favorite snacks is popcorn, which not only can be eaten, but can be the basis for an art project as well. When you make popcorn decorations, be sure to have extra popcorn for eating.

Popcorn Balls

 These are great party favors and everyone can help.

10 quarts of popped corn
1 cup molasses
1 cup sugar
2 tbs. butter or margarine

Put the popcorn in a large container. Measure molasses, sugar and butter into a three-quart saucepan. Cook, stirring occasionally, to crack stage, 273° to 274° on a candy thermometer. Drizzle mixture over popcorn, stirring to cover corn with the glaze. Be sure not to burn yourself; the mixture is very hot. After the glaze and corn are well mixed, grease your hands with butter or margarine and shape the popcorn mixture into medium sized balls (about 3 inches in diameter). Cover the balls loosely with waxed paper and keep at room temperature. This recipe makes about 3 dozen balls.

Caramel Corn

 This old favorite is a great treat.

1 cup brown sugar
½ cup butter or margarine
¼ cup light corn syrup
½ tsp. salt
½ tsp. baking soda
15 cups of popped corn
mixed nuts or peanuts (optional)

Mix sugar, butter, corn syrup and salt in a saucepan. Cook and stir over medium heat until the mixture bubbles around the edges. Cook an additional 5 minutes. Remove from heat and stir in baking soda until the mixture is foamy. Put popcorn into 2 greased 13x9x2-inch pans. Pour half the glaze mixture over the popcorn in each pan and stir until all the corn is covered with glaze. Bake at 200° for 1 hour. Stir in nuts while still hot, if desired. Cool and store in an air-tight container or plastic bag.

Popcorn Strings

 Stringing popcorn is simple and requires only items you normally have. All you need in addition to the popcorn is a darning needle or any other large needle with a sharp point, a spool of thread, a pair of scissors, a thimble, and a small 1-inch square of cardboard.

Cut the thread to the length you desire, or plan to tie several shorter lengths together. Push the needle through the cardboard square and secure with a knotted end. String the popcorn on the thread, pushing three or four kernels at a time down to the end.

Use strings of popcorn for the Christmas tree, or tie popcorn strings in a nearby tree for the birds.

Popcorn Paintings

You can make popcorn into mosaics. Using a paper or cardboard backing, trace an outline of an object: a tree, animal or bird, perhaps. Spread glue on a small area at a time. Glue the popcorn onto the backing. Color the popcorn with water colors, or color it before starting with food coloring.

9. HOLIDAY FUN AND ENTERTAINING

Meal times seem to be the focal point of getting together for family and friends. Seasonal and holiday themes are automatically set by our calendars, and family special events as well. Because families get together for special occasions, it is possible that your grandchildren will be visiting you on occasions when you entertain. They will enjoy helping with the planning and preparations for the happy event.

The formal dining room is not always the entertainment setting; any area in or outside the home may be used. When we write about the dining area, we are talking about the area where the food is being served.

MABEL, MABEL, SET THE TABLE

 Basic table setting can involve all of the grandchildren, nieces, nephews and other children. Give each a chore to be responsible for. Very young children can learn how to arrange the silverware, and how to place the forks, knives and spoons in their proper places. What a good way to practice counting! Older children can assist with napkin folding, place cards, centerpieces. Teenagers can assist with food preparation and perhaps care of the very elderly members of the family.

Set one place with utensils as an example for the young children to copy. Teach them that forks are placed to the left of the plate, with the dinner fork closest to the plate. Show them that the knives and spoons are placed to the right of the plate. Tell them that the utensils used first are placed furthest from the plate. Show them exceptions, such as butter knives, cocktail forks and spoons, if you plan to use them. Tell them that the cutting edge of the knives face the plate.

Add the stemware, coffee cups and plates to your sample setting for the children who will be setting the dishes on the table. Tell them the stemware and coffee cups should be placed above the knife and spoons. Show them that the bread and butter dishes should be placed above the forks. The napkin can be to the left of the forks if it is folded or in a napkin ring, or in any position that adds decoratively to the table setting. If folded decoratively, it might be on the plate or in a piece of stemware.

NAPKIN FOLDING

One of the things we were taught by our grandparents was napkin folding, which made the table a little more festive. Some of the examples we add are our favorites, and the one for which we received the most compliments is the Lotus Bowl. Napkin folding is easy and fun for even small children. It also keeps them busy and out from underfoot.

A Simple Roll in a Glass

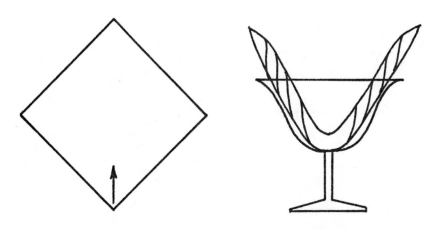

Start with a stiff, square cloth napkin. A sturdy paper towel will also work, but it must be square. Make a simple roll starting at one corner and roll the napkin into a tube. Fold the tube in half and insert it into a glass.

The Fan

Start with a stiff, square cloth napkin or a sturdy paper towel. First fold the napkin in half, and then make a series of accordion pleats. Grasp the bottom and twist; the top fans out automatically.

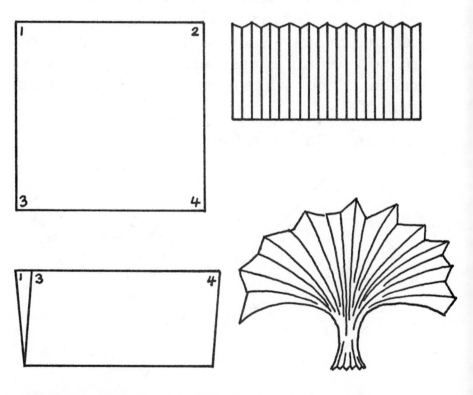

The Boat

 Start with a stiff, square cloth napkin. Fold it in half.

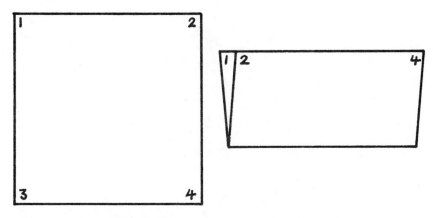

Fold it in half again. Fold it into a triangle. Put folded corner (5) at the top by raising it to meet the other corners (1, 2, 3, and 4).

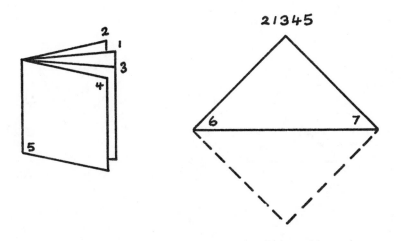

With your fingers, hold 1 through 6; fold 6 and 7 down to meet at the center.

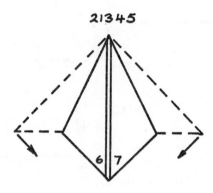

Turn over and fold 6 and 7 back. Then fold together so that 6 and 7 are touching.

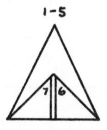

Grasp folded corners in one hand, turn over, and pull ends up one at a time to create the sails. Here is your finished product:

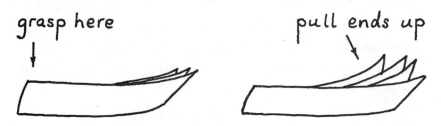

The Lotus Bowl

Start with a stiff, square cloth napkin. Fold each of the corners to meet in the center, reducing the size of the square.

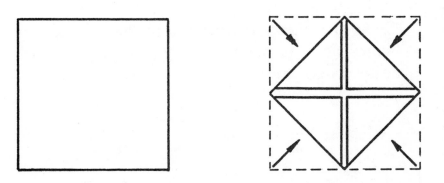

Fold each of the corners to meet in the center *two more times.* Then turn the napkin over and repeat the procedure one more time. The napkin will reduce in size each time.

Place your hand on the center of the folded napkin, and using your hand as a support, turn the napkin over. Take each corner at the center and gently peel it back over the reverse side, being careful not to peel it over all the way. Complete the process of pulling back each corner from the center, using continual support with one hand under the napkin.

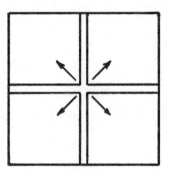

The finished product should look like a lotus cup. Fill with candy, favors, or simply put them on each plate as a decoration.

DECORATIONS FOR THE TABLE

In addition to setting out flatware, dishes and napkin folding, there are many different tasks associated with table setting that appeal to children of all ages. They include making place cards, centerpieces, and decorations for the room.

Place cards can be made in many different shapes. Let the kids be inventive. Give them colored paper, pens and ribbons. Encourage them to make place cards that carry the theme of the meal, whether it be a birthday, holiday or special celebrating. If the place cards are a special shape, show the children how to make a pattern to draw around, and then cut the shapes out with scissors. They may need help in spelling names and where to place the cards on the table. Make time to answer questions, or ask another family member or friend to help.

Centerpieces

Older children can arrange centerpieces using fresh or artificial flowers, candles, vegetables, seasonal leaves, commercially made items, or whatever seems decorative for the occasion. Try these ideas:

- When arranging the centerpiece, make sure that people are not hidden by the decoration. The centerpiece should have a low profile. If using taller objects, provide adequate "see-through" space to allow visual contact across the table.

- Use a clear decorative glass dish. Its shape can be round, oblong or square, but should be at least 3 inches deep. Fill it with water, using food dyes to color the water, and float candles. Floating candles are usually available in your neighborhood card shop, drug store or variety store. Leave enough room between candles to give them freedom to move freely when lit. This will give a very soft effect and will not interfere with the diners' vision.
- Add your own ideas to our list: cupids, Easter eggs, flags, flowers, Jack-o-lanterns, leaves, lilies, May poles and baskets, Menorahs, pine cones, pumpkins, shamrocks, turkeys, small Christmas trees.

IT'S PARTY TIME!

 What can be more festive than a party? Celebrating birthdays and anniversaries brings family members together. If it's a surprise party, kids are great secret keepers; don't fail to confide in them. Include them in party planning and preparation.

Party themes vary according to age, the occasion, and if the party is indoors or outdoors. Whether you choose to have it in a special location or at home, follow a general pattern of preparation:

- Select a theme.
- Plan the decorations to go with the theme.
- Select a menu.
- Select games to be played, or music, or other entertainment if you want it.
- Set a time that is comfortable for everyone.
- Plan clean-up.

Planning the party can be as much fun as the actual party. If you plan ahead in plenty of time, everything will be ready and there will be no last minute rushes or stress. Assign special jobs to the kids and make sure they know their responsibilities. They can, for example, make all the decorations. Encourage them to be creative — let those imaginations work!

Happy Birthday Parties, Penny Warner, New York, NY: St. Martin's Press, 1985

Better Homes and Gardens Blue Ribbon Bazaar Gifts, G. Knoz, ed., Des Moines, IA: Meredith Corp., 1987

You're Invited to a Party

 But first we need to make the invitations. Use white or construction paper, and cut invitations in imaginative shapes to go with your party theme. Star invitations are easy for a Christmas party, balloons for birthdays, or whatever fits.

Be sure to include the reason for the party, the time, the date and the location. You may want to include what dress is appropriate (it's a patio party: wear casual clothing) and you may request an answer (RSVP).

Provide paper, crayons, scissors, colored pens and glue sticks. You may need to help younger children address envelopes.

Party Decorations

 Is it a birthday party? Have the kids cut out stars and moons from shiny silver or gold paper, punch holes in them and string them to make a banner that can be hung in the room.

Make rocket favors. Color empty tissue holders with paint, or silver paper. Close off one end and fill with candy or plastic trinkets. Make a cone for the top by cutting a circle large enough to cover the tube, slitting one side, and adjusting it to fit. Tape it to the top of the tube. Make three paper fins for the bottom of the rocket — make a narrow fold on the edge and glue or tape the fold to the tube. Write a guest's name on the side of the tube.

Make a cake in the shape of a rocket or star, or decorate a sheet cake with a rocket.

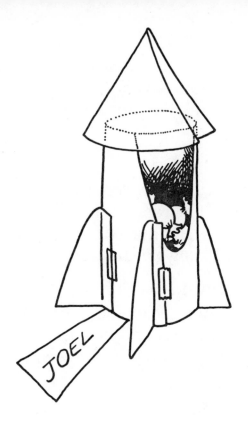

Cornucopia Favors

Cornucopias are traditional party favors or tree decorations. They can be made from stiff paper that has been cut into a circle with a slit from the perimeter to the center of the circle. Wrapping paper (one with a design that is appropriate for the celebration) works very well. Roll the paper to form a cone, glue the edges together, punch a hole in opposite sides of the cone and string a ribbon through the holes to act as a hanger. The cone can be filled with nuts, fruits, candy, small toys, coins, or whatever you desire. Names can be printed on the outside of the cones or numbers can be used and a lottery can be played for each cone. This is great fun when the cones are all filled with different items.

Candy Decorations

 Make gumdrop decorations for party trees or holiday trees. String the gumdrops with a needle and a strong thread. Tie the thread to a bow and hang on the tree.

More Birthday Ideas

Birthday themes can focus on the particular month of the birthday, or the special interest of the honored guest. Here are some ideas:

- camping trip
- clown party
- ice cream party
- zoo party
- theater party
- magic party
- slumber party
- presidents party
- pizza parlor party
- back-to-school party
- favorite sport party

Holiday Parties

Many holidays throughout the year lend themselves to decorating and party themes. Add holidays to the list that reflect your ethnic or religious background.

- New Year's Day and Eve
- Martin Luther King Day
- Mardi-gras
- Valentine's Day
- St. Patrick's Day
- April Fools' Day
- Easter
- May Day
- Mother's Day
- Father's Day
- Grandparent's Day
- The 4th of July
- Halloween
- Thanksgiving
- Christmas
- Hanukkah

EASTER EGG HUNTS

Easter egg hunts are fun for everyone, indoors or outdoors. If you leave candy and real eggs too long outdoors, you may lose some to local critters, so hide eggs just ahead of the hunt, or wrap carefully. Prizes don't have to be candy; they can be messages, or trinkets. Make rules so the hunt is fair for everyone.

Let your grandchildren make Easter egg prizes using empty shells; make a small hole in the shell and drain when you are making scrambled eggs or baking. Wash the egg inside carefully. When the shell is dry it can be painted or dyed and filled.

Kids can hide eggs for Grandma and Grandpa to find, too.

PARTY COSTUMES

Children enjoy dressing up and pretending to be someone else. The opportunity to wear a costume and to use their imaginations can be loads of fun. Some of the costumes they like most are witches, spooks and ghosts, scarecrows, princes and princes-ses, clowns, pirates and animals. Cats are a favorite for little girls; little boys like to be tramps or hobos.

Halloween is a favorite time to dress up in costume, but a costume party can be fun for a birthday or some other holiday. New Year's Eve is another favorite costume time.

Rummage through your closets and chests and we are sure you will find a wealth of materials to use for making costumes.

Making Masks

 Simple masks, best for tramps, bums and hobos, can be made of old nylon stockings. Use clear fingernail polish to draw circles or holes where you want to cut out the nose and eyes; it will keep down excessive runs. Keep the holes large enough to be functional but not so large that they destroy the effect. Black hose make the best masks, and opaque white stockings work very well, too.

Pillow case masks are easy to make but require some sewing for proper fitting. They can be shaped to the size of the child's head and a draw string around the base can make them easy to wear and take off. They can be dyed and painted, and faces or objects can be glued on for special effects.

Paper mache, string, or cheese cloth masks can be made ahead of time and fitted to the child's face and head. Blow up a balloon to about the size of the child's head and use it as the base for the mask. Cover the balloon with vaseline. Layer on paper strips, string or pieces of cheese cloth that have been dipped into glue or paste. Let the paper, string or cloth dry for a few days and deflate the balloon carefully. Do not pop the balloon: release the air slowly to avoid losing the shape of the mask. Cut openings for eyes, nose and mouth with an exacto knife or razor blade. Decorate the mask with paint, or glue on details.

Masks made out of paper bags are easiest and fastest to make. They require a bag slightly larger than the child's head and durable enough to be worn for a couple of hours. Do not use plastic bags.

Masks can be made from paper plates, which are easily painted or colored with crayons or marking pens. Pieces of other paper plates can be attached for ears; yarn hair can be glued on the edges.

Foil masks can be made using three or four thicknesses of aluminum kitchen foil. Press the foil against the child's face, making an exact replica. Remove and use scissors to cut out eyes, nose and mouth. Use transparent tape to add detail cut out of paper.

Halloween Costume Party

 Halloween is one of the favorite holidays for kids. A costume party for older children can be great fun. Have them make invitations and party favors. Organize some activities like ducking for apples, blind man's bluff and other party games. Older teens like dance parties, and you should have lots of goodies to eat. There can never be too much food for teens! Prior to the party put them to work making the cookies, sandwiches, punch, etc. Wear costumes yourselves and be part of the party. This will allow you to supervise what is happening without appearing to be a policeman.

Don't forget the camera! A polaroid is great, but video taping is wonderful. You will be able to show the tape at the end of the evening when energy is running out.

MAKING VALENTINES

Valentines can be made from stiff paper, construction paper, ribbons and bows, various types of cloth, paper doilies, old candy boxes, wrapping paper, and old greeting cards and valentines. Red paper is usually a must and can be purchased at most stationery stores. Encourage the kids to make up verses or poems for their valentines. A short message can be romantic or comical. Valentines can be simple hearts or very complicated, with moving parts.

GREETING CARDS

Everyone enjoys receiving a homemade greeting card, especially one made by a child. Birthdays, anniversaries, Mother's Day, Father's Day, Easter and many other days are occasions to send greeting cards. Sometimes no occasion is necessary: just "I miss you" is enough. They can be constructed from colored paper and cut into different shapes. Paper cut-outs pasted on white paper can be made from tracing pictures in magazines and books. Original drawings can be made, using colored pens and pencils, crayons, paints or colored inks.

If you have snapshots of family members, it's fun to add cut-outs of them to greeting cards. An actual photo of Mom can go on her Mother's Day card, for example.

If you have a computer, you can make interesting greeting cards; share your knowledge with the kids.

Object Greeting "Cards"

Other objects can be used as a form of greeting card, such as rocks for paper-weights, with the greeting painted or glued on, or pieces of wood decorated with greetings cut from old cards or decals and varnished. Let the kids say "Happy Birthday" in a different way.

CULTURAL THEMES FOR PARTIES AND GATHERINGS

Using cultural themes for get-togethers and parties gives children an opportunity to learn about people from other lands. Some good countries to begin with are Mexico, China and Japan, because there are many people from these countries living here, and food and items from their cultures are easy to find. If you and your grandchildren enjoy this activity, continue with other cultures.

In addition to finding recipes, make a library project out of it. Look up the country in books or encyclopedias. Find some pictures of arts or crafts that can give ideas about decorations for the table, or find things in local shops. If Grandma or Grandpa have a record with music from that country, play it during your party or dinner. Some libraries have records and tapes that can be checked out, and you may find appropriate music there. Here are some ideas from our close neighbor.

A MEXICAN PARTY

Mexican Placemats

 Make large pieces of heavy white paper available with colored pens, crayons and pencils for the children to decorate to fit the theme of your Mexican dinner. The children can draw sombreros, birds, a cactus, donkeys, flowers and other pictures that are commonly drawn on Mexican objects.

Mexican Foods

- Tacos or taquitos: shells can be purchased at your local crocery store. Soft tortillas are also available, and can be fried and made into a taco shell. Directions are on the package. If you are lucky and have a Mexican deli in your area, smaller taco shells can be made to order. They are easier to eat and make good hors d'oeuvres. Do you have a lazy Susan? Put it in the middle of the table with all the taco fillings: refried beans, ground meat seasoned with taco seasoning, shredded cheese, shredded lettuce, salsa, guacamole, and sour cream are common.

- Make Mexican-style hors d'oeuvres. Open a can of refried beans, add salsa and shredded cheese, heat and serve with taco chips.

- Make guacamole yourself. Buy ripe avocados (if not available, put unripened avocados in a paper bag, close it tight, and put it in a dark place for 2 to 3 days. Check for ripeness; they should be soft.) Peel the avocado and mash the fruit. Save the seed! (see *Avocado Plant*, page 26). Season to taste; choose from these seasonings: salt, garlic, chopped chiles, onions, salt, cilantro, parsley, chili powder, mayonnaise and sour cream. If you put the seed in the guacamole it will keep the dip from turning brown. A few drops of lemon juice also helps if you don't wish to show the seed in the dip. Use lemon juice sparingly to avoid changing the flavor.

- Finish the meal with a dessert that you and the kids made together.

Mexican Wedding Cakes

1 cup butter or margarine, softened
1 tsp. vanilla
2¼ cups flour
¼ tsp. salt
¾ cup finely chopped walnuts
½ cup confectioner's sugar

In a bowl, mixer bowl or food processor, mix ingredients together. Shape the dough into 1-inch balls (rolling the dough in your hands). Place on a greased baking sheet and bake 10 to 12 minutes at 400°. Remove from the oven and roll individually in a bowl of confectioner's sugar. Cool and roll a second time in the sugar. (You may need more sugar.)

Children also love these Mexican foods: homemade tortilla chips, nachos (chips with melted cheese), taco salad, refried bean dip, homemade salsa, Mexican style eggs (huevos rancheros), fajitas, tacquitos, tamales, enchiladas and chili rellenos. You can find recipes in the library if you don't have a cookbook that has them.

SWISS FONDUE PARTY

 Here's another good idea for a party with a theme from a different country. Fondue comes to us from Switzerland and is always enjoyed, especially by kids.

The New International Fondue Book, Robert and Coleen Simmons, ed., San Leandro, CA: Bristol Publishing Enterprises, 1990

Fill a fondue pot about half-full with equal amounts of oil and butter. (Or a less fattening method of cooking fondue is to use chicken or beef broth.) Prepare meat ahead of time by cutting into one-inch cubes. If you use chicken or fish, be sure the pieces are boneless. Cut vegetables into bite-sized pieces; zucchini, mushrooms, pearl onions, potato, sweet potato or yams, are good to use. Put each type of food into a separate bowl. You can also use meat balls, sausage pieces, clam strips, oysters and crab legs.

Include sauces to go with the "dippers." Some good ones include curried mayonnaise, sour cream with horseradish, sour cream mustard, Chinese sweet and sour sauce, and commercially made steak sauce.

If you don't have fondue forks, use wooden skewers purchased from your grocery store. If you use skewers, mark each one so the owner can identify his.

Use separate pots if cooking fish and meat at the same meal. Allow one pot for every 4 to 5 people. Preheat the oil to just below smoking, and cook each piece for a only a minute or two.

Have a salad ready to eat while the food is in the pot cooking. Or have a salad bar set up on a side table so that everyone can construct his own salad.

Swiss Chocolate Fondue

For dessert, Swiss chocolate fondue is perfect.

12 oz. chocolate (milk or semi-sweet
   baking chocolate work equally well)
3 tbs. cointreau, brandy or rum; or
   rum flavored extract
3/4 cup whipping cream

Melt chocolate with whipping cream in the top of a double boiler over hot but not boiling water, stirring while the mixture melts. Stir in liqueur or flavoring. Transfer to a fondue pot over low heat or a chafing dish.

Good dippers for chocolate fondue include strawberries, banana chunks, pineapple spears or cubes, pieces of apples and pears, and canned mandarin oranges. You can also dip cubes of pound cake, plain cookies or oatmeal cookies.

10. GRANDPARENT SPECIALTIES

What special things can your grandchildren do when they visit you that they may not do anywhere else? They will never forget these experiences.

THE MAGIC PURSE

An enchanted purse, or other container, always seems to know which grandchild or grandchildren are coming to visit, and always has a surprise for each one of them. It might be a coin, or a small treat, or a special eraser for the end of a pencil, or a plastic animal. The surprises are never expensive. When they arrive, the small children will give you a hello kiss and run for the Magic Purse!

TREASURE CHESTS

Grandma or Grandpa can have a "treasure chest" or a box that contains all the items they've saved for the little ones to explore or to use when visiting. Some suggestions for items are rocks, shells, corks, pictures, special books, old toys, coins, old hats, purses, wallets, jewelry or anything that might be interesting to small children. Items of clothing are great for playing dress-up. Be sure to take pictures! Your grandchildren will spend a lot of time in the treasure chest, hunting and seeking treasures. (Do not put anything of great value to you in the chest.)

Change items regularly as the children grow older. Old photo albums and old school yearbooks really interest older children. An occasional song sheet from years past or a scrapbook can be very entertaining.

More for the Treasure Chest

Include makeup, nontoxic paints or theatrical makeup in the treasure chest for an activity full of fun. Kids love making up, and you can join in. Some enjoyable makeup jobs include clown faces, animals and creature faces. These are fun to wear as well as paint on the kids. Simple makeup art is not difficult, and does not require a lot of artistic talent. Once made up, kids can act out a part. A candid picture will retain the image for posterity.

VIDEO TAPING

Making home videos can be loads of fun. If you have a camcorder, you have a valuable communication tool, and the transportability of the camera and the tape give endless possibilities. If you don't have one, seriously consider purchasing one for a record of your family gatherings as well as your own travels. Instead of letters or phone calls, a homemade video message along with a family celebration or vacation makes a wonderful exchange between distant family members. Copies can be made and tapes can be sent home with the kids. Some of the most entertaining videos are those that include dramas written by the kids, family outings, sport contests, etc.

Video Rentals

In addition to taking your own videos, there is a video rental shop in every neighborhood where you can pick out a special movie of interest to the children. It gives you a chance to turn off commercial TV and monitor what they watch.

And Video Games

 Home video games are popular. Their initial cost is high, but they have longevity. Many games are appropriate for all ages and some are highly educational. Nobody said learning can't be fun.

AUDIO TAPING

Children (and adults) are fascinated when they first hear their own voices on audio tape. "It doesn't sound at all like me!" A tape recorder can provide long hours of entertainment. It's inexpensive, portable, and the cassettes are also inexpensive and readily available. Recordings can be made from records, radios and other cassettes. With a microphone, personal messages can be recorded. Cassettes are small enough that they can be sent through the mail at a very reasonable cost.

Tape a story. Each person can take one or more characters from a familiar story, such as *Cinderella*. Or the kids can write and plan their own "radio shows." Some of the family's most hilarious memories can come from sessions like this. They can also interview family members and friends, record their own playing of musical instruments or singing. In addition to making your own tapes, there is a vast supply of commercial tapes available. Libraries loan books on tape. Many are now available for sale in supermarkets, drug stores, book stores and novelty shops.

The new audio playback machines are all equipped to use headphones that enable the user to listen to the tape without disrupting others. Many modern portable radios now have tape playing ability.

> *The Tape Recorder*, E.D. Ives, Knoxville, TN: The University of Tennessee Press, 1980
>
> *Tape Recording for the Hobbist*, A. Zuckerman, Indianapolis, IN: Howard W. Sams Co., 1977

Memories on Tape

 The tape recorder will give you a chance to give your grandchildren a very precious gift. When they are visiting, encourage them to ask you questions about your history: what it was like when you were a young child, where you lived, how you shopped, what school was like, what you remember about your own grandparents and other family members. When the children are not visiting you, take some extra time and tape as much as you are able to about your lives. The information you preserve in this way, and your own voices telling the stories, will be among the most valuable possessions your grandchildren will own. Perhaps you can do some of this on videotape.

MAKE A FAMILY TREE

 Make a family tree with your grandchildren. This project can be simple, or very complex, depending on the time you wish to give it.

Your local bookstore has interesting books that can help you with this valuable project. Put together a three-hole binder with your family tree; include sections for information about each of your ancestors. This is a project that may interest you as well as the children, and the information you collect will be a valuable family keepsake.

> *The Beginner's Ancestor Research Kit*, Phil Breck, San Leandro, CA: Bristol Publishing Enterprises, 1990
>
> *The Genealogist's Guide*, G. A. Marshall, Baltimore, MD: Genealogical Publishing Co., 1980

COLLECTING HISTORY

When a very newsworthy event occurs, such as a volcano erupting, a president dying, an earthquake, or the removal of the Berlin wall, help your grandchildren save front pages of newspapers, copies of news magazines, and other media keepsakes in a special place, such as a three-ring binder with plastic sleeves into which they can slip the paper or magazine. This will be an interesting treasure for the future.

FAMILY AMATEUR HOUR

Can Grandma or Grandpa play a musical instrument or sing? What special talents do your grandchildren have? This is the time to encourage the kids to perform. Old-fashioned songfests are fun. Each person can suggest a song that is one of his favorites. Plan ahead: get the kids to look up the words to their favorite songs and

write them down, later to be distributed to everyone. Try some old songs from the '30s and '40s, such as *MaresEatOats*, *Three Little Fishies*, the *Hut Sut Song*, and many others. The kids love learning the words. Old rooter's cheers and yells are fun. Looking up the words to old songs can be a great research library project for older grandchildren.

MAKE UP STORIES

Our grandfather used to tell us about the Rock Candy Mountain and the Lemonade Springs. To this day, we still remember those stories. Make up special stories to tell your grandchildren about a special adventure, or an animal, or embellish a story that you remember.

PETS

 Do you have a pet? Share some background information about your pet. Use an encyclopedia to teach grandchildren about the pet's historical origins and development.

Caring for your pet is a major chore. Knowing what it should eat, how much, and how often is important for the pet's health and longevity. Teach the children, and encourage them to help keep the pet's environment healthy and clean.

Pet's Magazine, Moorshead Publications, 1300 Don Mills Road, Don Mills, Ontario, Canada M3B 3M8

CORRESPONDENCE

 Unless you are lucky enough to live very close to your grandchildren, they may not have the opportunity to visit often. Make a habit of corresponding with them on a regular basis. Include interesting items you have clipped from newspapers and magazines, stories you have heard, and news about yourselves. Don't let the letters get into an "I am fine; how are you" rut; that will bore you and the reader. Challenge the children by making mistakes in your letters which they must correct; send them riddles and problems that they must figure out; they'll have good reason to return a letter.

When the children are too young to read and write, send a short letter that can be read to them by Mom or Dad, and include a picture that you've clipped from a magazine or old book. Glue the picture on a blank recipe card, and write a comment or question on it. "What color are the bunny's eyes?" "How many buttons can you count?" "Grandpa loves you." We know children who treasure their "Grandma cards" and carry them wherever they go.

WHAT'S YOUR NAME AGAIN?

Call Me Ralph

Let your grandchild choose a different name to use for the whole day. You must remember to call him his new name — think up a penalty for error.

Role Playing

Pretend you are the characters in a favorite TV program. Spend all day role-playing the same characters.

11. ARTS, CRAFTS AND PROJECTS

There are so many arts and crafts that you can share with your grandchildren, we will not be able to mention them all. But we've done our best to give you many ideas, and both you and the kids will be able to add more. These activities require preparation and clean-up. Between visits from the children, save empty milk cartons, empty thread spools, empty cereal boxes including small individual sizes, orange juice cans, paper towel rolls, toilet tissue rolls, salt containers, odds and ends of yarn, scraps of string, pieces of fabric and other discards that you think might be useful. A box of brads to hold things together is a good idea, as well as tape and paper clips. Have a pair of blunt scissors for each of the young children.

Each child can have his own art supplies in a shoe box marked with his name. Include scissors, colored marking pens, white glue, crayons, colored pencils, a ruler and other useful items.

For many projects, a cover-up is necessary. One of the best is one of Grandpa's old shirts put on backwards with the collar cut off or tucked under, and the sleeves rolled up. Kids love to wear Grandpa's shirts, even the big kids.

Sunset Children's Crafts, Menlo Park, CA: Lane, 1976

Box Projects

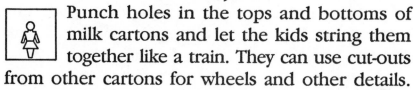 Punch holes in the tops and bottoms of milk cartons and let the kids string them together like a train. They can use cut-outs from other cartons for wheels and other details. Brads can hold parts together.

Airplanes, trucks, doll beds and other doll furniture can be made from cartons and thread spools. A salt box with the side cut out makes a good cradle; half of the box makes a good round table, with thread spools for stools. Bits of material can cover the tops of the stools. Start the children off with an example or two and see what they can create on their own.

PAINTING

Create an art center: choose a specific location where supplies can be stored and available for use when needed. An easel is wonderful, but a table is fine. A good way to make an easel is to cut a large cardboard box diagonally. Cut two slots on the top edge for clothespins to hold paper (see diagram).

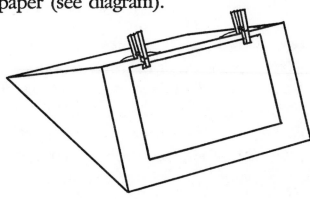

Use small milk cartons or juice cans for paint cans. Tempera paints are easily mixed and the easiest to clean up with soap and water. A large sheet of wrapping paper or butcher paper can serve as the canvas.

You can buy large brushes at a variety store or an art supply store. Let children try painting with old toothbrushes for a different effect.

You might want to cover the floor to catch drips, and cover the children as well. Large plastic aprons are the best. Avoid using newspapers on the floor, as the ink may come off on the floor and children's shoes. A large inexpensive plastic drop cloth can be purchased for very little money at a local hardware or variety store, or use an old plastic tablecloth. If the children are given instruction, they can be productive and neat. You do not need to be messy to be artistic.

Finger Painting — or Foot Painting

Finger painting is always fun for children, but it is messy, so be prepared for clean-up. For a *really* exciting artistic adventure, let them try painting with their feet!

Painting with Eye Droppers

Your pharmacist has eye droppers for sale. Your grandchildren will enjoy using them with tempera paints to make interesting designs. Another way to use eye-droppers: cut a 4-inch square of paper, use the eye-dropper to drop a splash of paint right in the middle of the paper, fold it in half, and then in half again. Unfold the paper to find the interesting design!

Plastic Foam Prints

 Save plastic foam containers that meat is sold on; wash them carefully. Cut off the sides to make a flat piece of foam. Begin with an original drawing, or a drawing that has been traced from a book or magazine. Tape the drawing to the foam so it will not move, and trace over it with a ball point pen, pressing down to make lines in the plastic foam. Remove the drawing. Apply tempera paint to the foam, covering it all. While it is still wet, put a clean piece of paper over the foam. Rub it all over with your hand. Lift it off — and there is a lovely print of your drawing!

Painting by the Numbers

 Painting by the numbers is a challenge for older children, who have to read and follow the directions in the painting kit.

Family Mural

 Tear a long sheet from a roll of wrapping or butcher paper, and stretch it out on a long table or on the floor (if you put it on the floor, you may need to put a large piece of cardboard under it). Use crayons, colored pencils, marking pens — anything you wish — and let everyone participate, even Grandma and Grandpa. You will be amazed at what can be created.

Finger Painting — Finger-Licking Good

Want to keep your little ones busy with a little extra treat? Cover them up, prepare an instant pudding of chocolate, vanilla or any other flavor, and then have them make a finger painting on the shiny side of a piece of freezer wrap. Not only is the art fun, but it has the added advantage of being finger-licking good! Have everybody help with clean up, as it can get messy.

GLITTER PAINTING

Put white glue in a saucer or a margarine tub. Use a paint brush to paint a design with glue on paper, and then shake glitter from dispensers onto the glue. You can buy glitter in dispensers in many colors at a craft store, and sometimes a variety store. This is also a good way to decorate gift wraps. A greeting or a person's name can be written with glue, and then covered with glitter.

Be prepared to vacuum up after this one!

SOAP SCULPTURE

Tell the children they *must not rub their eyes* when they work on this project. Mix 2 cups of laundry soap (not detergent) with water, a small amount at a time, until the mixture is the texture of a soft snowball. Let the children form the mixture into shapes; dry the shapes on pieces of waxed paper. After it has hardened, you can shape it further with a spoon if desired.

BAKER'S CLAY

Baker's clay is easy to make. Using a large mixing bowl, combine 1½ cups of water and 1 cup of salt. Add 4 cups of flour and mix until it forms a sticky paste. Knead until smooth. A food processor or bread dough mixer will make the chore easier and faster. If kneading by hand, do it to music with a beat, and the kids can keep time to the music while kneading. If the dough is too crumbly, add a few drops of water; if too sticky, add a little more flour. When finished, use the dough immediately or seal it in a plastic bag and refrigerate.

Baker's Clay Art

Baker's clay can be used to make a number of shapes and designs. Roll the dough out on a large sheet of aluminum foil with a rolling pin so the dough is about ¼-inch thick. Use cookie cutters or cut shapes out with paper patterns. Dough can be layered, using water for glue.

When all the cut-outs are made, place them on a teflon cookie sheet and bake at 300° for about 1½ hours, turning once after about 45 minutes. Times are approximate due to differences in ovens. Shapes should be rock hard when finished baking. After they cool, they can be painted and decorated. After painting, a coat of clear nail polish will preserve the pieces for posterity.

POTATO AND OTHER VEGGIE PRINTS

Cut a potato in half, and carve a design with a sharp knife or an exacto knife. Use an inked stamp pad for color, or put a little bit of tempera paint in a saucer, and make a print design on a paper or cloth. Use other interesting cut vegetables, such as half a bell pepper, half a Brussels sprout, half a mushroom, a length-wise slice of broccoli, and an apple cut at right angles to the core. Erasers work in place of vegetables, and so do pieces of sponge. This is also a great way to make individualized gift wrap.

MOBILES

Mobiles can be constructed with string or fish line and thin wooden dowels, hangers, pieces of wood lath, wires, wooden chop sticks or any other materials that act as frames. Attach folded paper decorations (see *Origami*, page 49), paper cut-outs, decorated egg shells, wire sculptures, or other light-weight items with string or fish line. Make sure each item can move freely on your moving sculpture.

Designing and Constructing Mobiles, Jack Wiley,
Blue Ridge Summit, PA: Tab Books, 1985

PLASTER ART

If you're going to the beach, this is a good craft activity to take along. And if you're not, put some sand in a dish pan and do it in the back yard, or on the porch. All you need is plaster of paris, which you will mix with water, and your imagination. Remember that plaster of paris will block drains. Mix it in disposable containers such as coffee cans so you can throw the whole works in the trash when you finish.

Make a shape, an indentation, in damp sand, and put in pebbles or other small decorations to make your design (you might make a fish, and have a colored stone for an eye). Mix plaster of paris according to package instructions, and pour enough into the sand to fill your design. Put a loop of wire into the top of the plaque for a hanger while the plaster is still wet. Give it time to harden, and you have an imaginative decoration for your wall. You can paint it, if you like, or leave it white.

If you do not wish to do sand casting, use a disposable aluminum pie tin. First grease the tin with petroleum jelly, and lay pieces of string, yarn, old jewelry, or other decoration on the plate (remember, the part that faces down on the plate will be the part that will appear when your figure is unmolded). Carefully pour liquid plaster of paris over your decorations until the pan is full. Again, add a loop of wire to the top of the plaque before it dries.

Hand Prints

Grease a disposable aluminum pie plate and pour in enough plaster of paris to fill it half full. Then have your grandchild spread his fingers and make his hand print in the wet plaster of paris. Include a wire hanger at the top of the circle while it is still wet. The child's name can carefully be written in the wet plaster under the hand print. When the plaster dries, it can be painted around the edges of the hand, or decorated with decals, and then varnished. It makes a great gift for Mom or Dad; even better if each child does one, for a personalized collection for the wall.

GIFT MAKING IDEAS

Gifts made by the kids while they are visiting with you provide joy for everyone. There is special pleasure in making something for someone, and special pleasure in receiving a hand-made gift. Here are some ideas for your grandkids:

- Make a picture frame, or buy an inexpensive one to decorate, and include a photograph of yourself with the recipient.
- Buy a light switch cover for the bedroom or any other room, and decorate it with paints, or use glue to cover it with special fabric.
- Cover a metal or plastic wastebasket with felt

and decorate it with yarn, buttons, scraps of materials or cut-outs of clowns, ships, dolls, airplanes, sports figures, etc. Coat with clear plastic varnish.

- Make napkin rings with felt and decorate with sequins, lace, jewels, or paper cut-outs.
- Make a calendar for the coming year from an existing calendar. Replace art with personal art. Add information on the appropriate dates that is meaningful to the receiver, such as birthdays or anniversaries of family members, graduations, etc.
- Make a recipe book of all your favorite recipes for goodies everyone in the family loves. Use your own handwriting and add your own art.
- Make pencil and pen holders out of juice cans or other small cans. They can be decorated in the same manner as the wastebaskets, even in matching styles. The bottom of the cans should be painted or covered with material. Cover with a coat of clear plastic varnish. You can use small bottles or jars in the same manner; cover the bottom with felt to guard against breakage.
- Yarn flowers can be made into a simple bouquet. You need one skein of yarn and a piece of cardboard 4-5-inches square for small flowers, and larger for larger flowers. Wind the yarn around the cardboard, one loop next to the other, until the cardboard is

covered. Carefully slip the loops off the cardboard and tie securely in the center. Snip off the loose ends from the center tie. Pull each loop out to the side, making a round flower head, and fluff up. You can attach a long wire to the flower for a stem, or glue the flower onto a decorated bottle, wastebasket or pencil holder. Add sequins for the centers, or use bits of colored ribbon. This makes a very professional-looking gift that will be cherished for many years.

Better Homes and Gardens Blue Ribbon Bazaar Crafts, G. Knox, ed., Des Moines, IA: Meredith Corp., 1987

Gifts You Can Make Yourself, Sunset Books, Menlo Park, CA: Lane, 1965

GIFT WRAPPING

Teaching the kids how to wrap a gift takes time and patience, but once mastered, it is a skill with great value, especially when help is needed at holiday time! Start by teaching them how to fold the paper around the corners of the package. The next challenge is learning how to tie the package for an attractive appearance.

Buy some spools of different colored ribbon and teach the kids how to make bows. Many ribbon containers have directions on the package. Get the kids to make a whole bag of bows to be saved and used at a later date. See *Potato Prints*, page 145, for ideas for making gift wrap.

Creative Gift Wrapping, P. Kirby, New York: Weidenfeld and Nicholson, 1987

BIRD FEEDER

Buy suet from your butcher. Roll a pine cone in the suet and then roll the cone in bird seed. Tie a string around the top of the cone and hang it in a tree close to a window, so you can enjoy watching the birds eat. After they have nibbled it clean, replenish it with more suet and seeds.

BOOK MAKING

Children love to make books. They can make scrapbooks of pictures they have collected; they can write stories which they have illustrated; they can make small photo albums of a trip, or of their pet or other experience. All they need are sheets of paper of a uniform size, heavier sheets for back and front covers, and yarn, or staples, or other means of holding the book together.

JEWELRY MAKING

Homemade jewelry is always appreciated when it is received as a present. See more about jewelry in *Hobbies*, page 75.

Copper-Enameled Jewelry

Copper-enameling is easy to do and not costly. It does require a small electric kiln, which can be purchased from a hobby shop. The shop also sells precut copper pieces and ground colored glass. The ground glass is easily applied. Results are professional, and the jewelry can be worn with pride.

Beads

Stringing beads to make necklaces, bracelets and earrings is easy for every age. Beads are available at sewing centers, novelty shops, discount stores, hobby shops and craft shops.

TISSUE PAPER ART

Paper Roses

Cut out tissue in the shape of large petals, 4-6 inches across, several at a time, and roll around a pencil from the bottom up. They can be in various sizes. Squeeze the tissue together on the pencil and then unroll. Separate the tissues and roll one at a time around the eraser end of the pencil, overlapping them carefully. Slip the rose off the pencil and tape the end. Add a wire for a stem.

Mexican Flowers

 Cut circles from different colors of tissue paper, 4-6 inches in diameter. Make 5 layers, choosing colors that you like, and cut 2 holes next to each other in the center of the stack. Put a long pipe cleaner into one hole and out the other, and twist together to make a stem. Fluff up the paper to look like a flower.

Crumpled Tissue Collage

 Using small pieces of paper, crumple them into small balls, and glue the balls onto a piece of paper with white glue.

Paper Collages

 You may use colored tissue, or dye your own tissue with water colors. You need a shallow pan and several layers of tissue paper. If you use colored tissues, which are not colorfast, the water can become the dye for other sheets of tissue. Place the first sheet of tissue flat on the shallow pan and sprinkle water over it. Cover with a second piece and continue until you have a pile of all the tissue you will need. Let the paper rest after you have drained away the water, and just before it is dry, separate the pieces to dry by themselves. Each sheet will be slightly different than the others, but the same colors will be prominent throughout the stack. Several colors may be applied at the same time, giving a mottled effect.

Glue torn or cut pieces of tissue to a plain paper backing to achieve the design you want. Save the most beautiful for framing.

SEED PAINTINGS

 Seeds come in various colors, sizes and shapes and can make an interesting effect when used for a "painting." Collect seeds from your garden or during your nature hikes, or buy seed packets from your nursery. You can also use seeds from your spice rack.

The first step is designing a drawing on paper. Do it in pencil; it does not have to be too elaborate. Or trace it from an existing picture. Glue the drawing to a piece of solid material, such as wood or cardboard. What you use depends on how you will display the finished product.

Next, make a number of cone dispensers, one for each type of seed. Coffee filters made good cones and they are easy to use. You can make your own cones out of stiff paper if you wish.

With an artist's brush dipped in glue or rubber cement, trace carefully over the drawing only where you want the seed to show. Sprinkle the seed onto the glue and let it dry. When dry, shake off the excess seed. You may have to repeat this process to get the proper effect. Do only one section of the drawing and one kind of seed at a time. Continue until the painting is completed. You may spend several days on this project.

Finally, cover with an acrylic plastic sheet, if framing, or varnish with clear plastic varnish.

SAND PAINTING

Sand painting has long been an American Indian art form. If you travel through the Southwest you will see all kinds of this art being displayed. Sand painting has a short life, unless an adhesive is used, and then it becomes a difficult task.

Most brickyards or building supply stores have clean white sand in stock. Use food coloring or vegetable dyes to color the sand. Painting can be done with the hands, but they must be dry. Cones can be used to regulate the flow of sand. An old funnel will work very well.

Use a piece of paper to draw a design, and lay it on a flat surface, such as a tray, or a cookie sheet, or a piece of wood. Then, using different colors of sand, follow the design you have made on paper.

Work outdoors out of the wind, or indoors with something covering the floor to keep the project from spreading all over the house. Have a camera ready to take a picture of the masterpiece when it is finished. Add the sand to the garden, or save it for another time.

See *Quiet Diversions*, page 50, for more sand art.

PAPER CHAINS

Paper chains are easy to make and can be used to decorate a room for a party, or to decorate a Christmas tree. Cut pieces of construction paper 1 inch by 4 inches. Using white glue or a glue stick, stick one end of the paper to the other, making a loop. Fit the next piece of paper through the loop and join it together the same way. Make the chain as long as you like.

BEAN BAGS

Bean bags are easy to make and are fun to use for tossing games. They can be made from almost any fabric and filled with beans or rice. The simplest shape is a square, but any design or shape can be made as long as it can be easily stitched around the edge, tightly enough to keep the rice or beans from leaking out.

Paint numbers on containers, such as coffee cans or plastic margarine tubs, and place them on one side of the room, perhaps in a circle with the largest number the "bull's eye." The game can be played by everyone according to agreed-upon rules. Keep score and declare a winner when a given number of turns or points have been reached.

HAND PRINTED SWEATSHIRTS

 Buy a plain light colored cotton T-shirt or sweatshirt. Wash and dry the shirt and iron out the wrinkles.

For a printing implement, use a large potato. Cut the potato in half, and using a paper pattern you have created, cut a four-leaf clover, a heart, diamonds, or any design you think will work. If you can't think of a design, look through magazines or art books for inspiration. You will need a potato printer for each color and each shape in your design. Trace the design on the cut side of the potato, using a knife with a sharp point. Cut about ¼-inch deep, and cut away the excess background, leaving a raised surface.

Use fabric paints or acrylic paints for printing. Paint the color on the potato with a brush, or pour a small amount of paint into a shallow container and dip the potato into the paint. Do not overload the potato with paint. Practice on a piece of paper or scraps of fabric before starting.

Carefully measuring, mark the sweatshirt with pencil where you want the design to go. Place a piece of freezer wrap inside the sweatshirt and pin it in place to keep the paper from slipping. Print one side of the sweatshirt and make sure the paint is completely dry before printing the other side.

If you want to paint sayings like, "I Love You, Mom" or "Here Comes a Big Hug," you will need to cut a stencil out of freezer paper. Attach the stencil with tape or pins to the area where you want the design, and paint over the stencil with a brush and fabric paint. What a great gift!

GIMP AND REED BRAIDING

 From commercial gimp or wild reeds, braided jewelry, lanyards, key rings and other useful items can be made. Gimp can be purchased at hobby shops, craft shops and toy stores. Wild reeds can be found near water, alongside lakes and streams. Braid as you would braid hair, and make rope-like strands to shape into finished items. Suggestions can be found at your local craft shop or library. The items you produce also make nice gifts.

COPPER ART

 Copper art is easy to do and produces a terrific-looking result. You can get sheets of copper foil from your craft store in many different sizes. You will also need copper sulfate and some fine (grade 00) steel wool.

Begin with an original drawing or something that has been traced from a book or magazine. Tape the picture on the copper so it won't move around, and put the copper, picture side up, on a small (1 inch) stack of newspaper. Trace the picture with a ball point pen. Press hard. Then take the paper off and redo all the lines so they are deep and easily seen from the other side.

Mix copper sulfate according to package directions: this requires adult supervision. Copper sulfate produces a strong odor, so go outdoors for this step. Mix the copper sulfate in a disposable pan large enough to hold the copper sheet.

Soak the copper sheet in the solution until it turns black. Put it on newspaper to dry. Then rub the foil with the steel wool, leaving the raised areas shiny and the background dark.

You can frame your picture, or mount it on material such as broadcloth or burlap. Makes a good gift.

CLOTH COLLAGES

 Using scraps of cloth as if they were paper, mount them with white glue in designs of choice on a large sheet of plain paper.

TILE PROJECTS

 Use leftover pieces of tile or purchase small tiles from a building supply or tile store. Discontinued tile is often on special sale and can be purchased for very little. Tile comes in all sizes and shapes, and can also be scored with a diamond cutter and broken or nipped with tile cutters to make even more shapes to fit your project.

Use small tiles of 1 inch or less to make coasters and trivets, covering jar lids and small container tops from cottage cheese. Metal lids work best, but plastic can be used.

Use large pieces up to 6 inches for making placemats, covering small table tops, and for hot plate stands.

Very large pieces, 12 inches or larger, can be used on bench seats, large counter tops and work benches.

A combination of all sizes can be used as pieces of art for wall decorations or table tops. You can cover part of your garage or basement wall with tile. Get inventive and make a design out of the scraps.

All of these projects are easy to do and require little or no prior experience. Use tile mastic to adhere the tile to the backing; it can be purchased at your building supply or tile store. Grout comes in all colors and can be purchased at the same place. Follow the instructions on the package for mixing and applying.

WALLPAPER ART

Visit your local wallpaper store and ask if they have any discontinued books of wallpaper samples. They also have remnants for sale at very little cost. Using wallpaper odds and ends, white glue and scissors, the kids can make collages, scenes, abstracts, cover bottles, pails, wastepaper baskets, and decopage wooden plaques and boxes. Picture frames can be covered with wallpaper — some of it is quiet elegant, such as foil or suede wallpaper.

TIN CAN TELEPHONES

This simple project is simple and will provide hours of fun. All you need is some string and two tin cans. Start with a piece of cotton string about 20-40 feet long. Punch a very small hole in the bottom of each of two well-cleaned and dried tin cans which have the labels removed. Be sure the open ends are smooth and free of jagged metal. Feed one end of the string through the bottom of one can from the inside and tie some knots on the string to keep it from being pulled through the can. Thread the string through the outside of the remaining can and knot it on the inside. The kids must keep the string taut when conversing, and the cans can be used both as a mouth piece and receiver.

STENCILING

 The art of stenciling came to us from ancient China. During the Middle Ages in Europe, stencils were very popular and evidence of their use can still be seen on church walls and old public buidings. Alphabet stencils can be purchased at most stationery stores. Stencils are easy to make; you need stiff paper, cardboard or a sheet of heavy plastic. Trace designs on the paper and cut them out with a sharp knife. Tape the stencil on the object you wish to decorate so that it will not move, and brush inks or paints over it.

Stencils can be used to make wrapping paper, decorate boxes, make individualized stationery, and produce signs, among other things (see *Sweatshirt Art*, page 156). You do not have to be an accomplished artist to construct a beautiful design.

PUPPET MAKING

Puppets can be simple or complex, but making them is always fun. Some of the more simple ones can be made from old

socks, knitted sweaters, colored shirts and other cloth remnants. Using a sock, divide the toe end into two parts with a small seam. Fingers can be put into one part and the thumb into the other. Paint on a face, or sew button eyes, if you wish. Use a sweater sleeve or shirt sleeve which has been seamed across the bottom in the same manner.

Puppets with heads and faces are more fun, but also require more skill to make. A broken doll or discarded stuffed animal can be reclaimed as a puppet. Hobby shops sell puppet faces; you must add material to finish these puppets.

Anything that can be operated by one hand will work. A famous actor on television used to paint a face on his hand, using his forefinger and thumb for the mouth, with a couple of eyes painted near the knuckle of the forefinger for the rest of the face. Try this one with Grandma's lipstick for the mouth and an old eyebrow pencil for the eyes and eyebrows.

Another simple puppet to construct is a lunch-bag puppet. Paint or crayon a face on the bottom surface while it is still folded flat. Insert a tongue and dress the bottom of the bag with arms, feet and clothing, painted, crayoned or glued on.

After puppets have been made, make a stage from a large cardboard box. You can add a dowel or a string to hang handmade curtains. Then encourage your grandchildren to make up a play. They can write a script, and even use a tape player for background music. This project will involve a number of rehearsals. When the whole project is completed, it's *Showtime*, with a performance for the family.

WIRE SCULPTURE

Use a piece of wood for the base; the size of the wood depends on the size of the sculpture that will be created. Drive a nail into the wood, leaving 2/3 of the nail above the wood. Wrap one end of a piece of wire securely around the nail, and then bend remaining wire into any desired shapes and designs. Or attach objects such as a flower head to the top of a shorter piece of wire.

You can also use a large cork for a base, if your sculpture is not too heavy.

SCRAP SCULPTURE

 Using scraps of material, cloth, wood, metal, vegetables, rocks, shells, bones, corks, tile, glass, tin cans or paper cartons, the children can create sculptures. Here are examples:

Clown Sculpture

Make a clown out of a potato head. Peel the potato partially for the face, and make features with pieces of dried fruit and vegetables stuck on the potato with straight pins. Use scraps of yarn or steel wool for the hair. Make the body of cloth and the hands and feet from cork. Use an old hacksaw blade which has been inserted into a slit in a piece of wood for a stand, or make a wire stand such as you did in *Wire Sculpture*.

Unfortunately it won't last forever, since the vegetables will wilt!

Witch Sculpture

Use a tennis ball and a twig with branches to simulate arms and legs to make fearsome witch. Attach the ball for the object's head, puncturing the ball to attach it to the twig. Paint a face on the ball. Use corks for hands and feet. You can even use a piece of cork for a nose, pinning it to the ball with a straight pin. Attach a black paper cone to the ball for a hat, and drape black material over the twig for a witch's dress. For a base, drill a small hole in a piece of wood and insert the body twig.

WEAVING

 Weaving can be done with yarn, a large yarn needle and a piece of cardboard, or with an elaborate floor loom, or with a variety of looms between the two extremes.

Cut an 8-inch square of stiff cardboard. Cut small incisions around the edge every ¼-inch, cutting into the cardboard about ½-inch with each incision. Then string the cardboard loom: with a length of yarn, go back and forth from one side of the cardboard to the other, looping the yarn on each edge around a "finger" of cardboard which you have created between incisions, until you have covered the square of cardboard. Thread the yarn needle with yarn; weave the yarn over and under the strands until you have come to the other edge. Loop the yarn around a "finger" of cardboard, turn it and weave the yarn to the other edge, going over the strand you went under the last time, and under the strand you went over the last time. When the cardboard has been completely covered, remove the square of fabric from the cardboard, and attach it to other squares to complete a project.

Toy stores and hobby shops sell small square looms that work approximately the same way. Also check your yellow pages under "Weaving."

HOOKING RUGS

 A latchet hook is easy to use, and children will enjoy hooking a small rug or wall hanging. A rug hooked in this manner is hooked from the front, and does not require a frame. Buy rug backing from your yard goods store. A design can be made on a piece of paper the size of the backing. Place the rug backing over the material and use indelible marking pens to produce the design on the backing. Use leftover odds and ends of yarn to fill in the design with the latchet hook.

You can also buy rug kits that require a latchet hook.

Rugs can be hooked with a punch needle from the back, using burlap or canvas backing which is attached to a frame. This is a little more difficult than latchet hooking, and you cannot see the finished product as you work.

And More and More

Your library shelves are loaded with books about arts and crafts we haven't mentioned, such as working with plastic, tin can art, leather crafts, needlepoint, stained glass art, batik, wood carving and whittling, quilting, metal crafts, book binding, basket-weaving, macrame, candle-making, framing. Explore the books with your grandchildren and find something fun to do. It's impossible to be bored!

12. AWAY FROM HOME

We've included day-trips in our *Outdoor Activities* chapter, but here are some ideas for longer trips with your grandchildren.

TRAVELING IN THE CAR

If you plan to take a car trip with your grandchildren, you will need to plan ahead. Pack a surprise bag with toys, games, crayons, coloring books, paper and stickers, and any other entertaining ideas you can think of. Pack another bag with food and snack items. Include crackers, cheese, veggies, graham crackers and other nutritional items. Drinks can be packed in a small cooler. Napkins, paper cups and handi-wipes are a necessity. Or pack individual bags, if children would prefer their own. If you are taking a long trip, plan ahead for a rest stop and a picnic lunch. Don't forget a little bag and trash containers.

A blanket and pillows can make the trip more comfortable. Try not to drive more than two hours without stopping for rests and a stretching session. Not only is this practice good for the kids, but it is also good for Grandma and Grandpa.

A car trip is a good time to have a sing-along or play license plate games. Who can find the most states? The most personal plates? Assign each one a number from one to nine, and the winner is the first one to total ten or twenty of that number. If there are only two kids, they can take numbers one to four and six to nine with five being a "wild" number. Or give each one a series of numbers, and the first to total fifty or one hundred is the winner.

Letters can also be used. The first one to spell a given word wins. Count the people in passing cars.

Count hawks, or special cars, or certain kinds of trucks. Make up your own rules.

Teach the children how to read the road map. Let them help you trace your trip, and follow your progress as you go.

Best Travel Activity Book Ever, Chicago, IL: Rand McNally, Inc., 1985

Audio Books

 Borrow books on tape from your library before you take your car trip, and spend the entire trip enthralled at the fascinating book of your choice. You can choose a classic, like *Treasure Island*, or a mystery, or an adventure story. The trip will fly by, and if you get to your destination too soon, everyone will want to stay in the car to hear the rest of the book!

Another Good Car Game

 Who am I? (Or What am I?) This question and answer game is great for the car, and good for a rainy day in the house, too. Everyone can play, and the questions can be adjusted to the ages of the children. One person is "It," and the others ask questions to start the game. "It" can only answer yes or no. The one who guesses the answer is the new "It." Possible questions:

Are you a person? place? or thing? Are you an animal? mineral? vegetable? Are you as big as a footstool? a house? Are you soft? hard? smooth? Are you round? square?

Make your own rules about numbers of questions or time limits. This mind-stretcher will make the children think.

License Plate Sayings

Make up sayings from the letters on license plates you see: JGM might be "just got married," SMR might be "slow motor rear," etc.

Alphabet Travel

Beginning with A, each person must find a sign that begins with each letter of the alphabet; the winner is the first to get to Z.

Add-On Stories

Anyone starts a story and the next one continues it. Anyone can end it, but it must be a logical ending. Another good way to spend time on the road.

GRANDTRAVEL

This company arranges very special trips for grandparents and their grandchildren. Tours are escorted, and planned carefully for private time alone together, and time for peer activities, to give adults a little breather. Each tour is designed to appeal to both generations. Current offerings in the U.S. include Washington, D.C., American Indian Country, The Grandest Canyons, Western Parks, California's Pacific Coast, and Alaska.

Foreign trips include Castles of England and Scotland, Holland's Waterways and Canals, France, Italy, a Kenya Safari and Australia. Call or write for their exciting brochure.

Grandtravel, 6900 Wisconsin Avenue, Suite 706, Chevy Chase, MD 20815 (800) 247-7651 or in Maryland, (301) 986-0790.

AIR TRAVEL

 When traveling by air, try to get a seat where no one is in front of you, next to the bulkhead or exit. They have more space for your legs and are easier to move in and out of. Take along a game bag such as you might in a car. Take some chewing gum to ease the pressure in the children's ears during take-offs and landings. Flight attendants are super with children and will help you with whatever is necessary.

WHALE WATCHING

 This is such an exciting experience, we include it even though it requires a trip to the West Coast during the migrating season. For actual dates, contact your travel agent. There are other sea animals that can be viewed at the same time, including dolphins, seals, sea lions, walrus and elephant bull seals. Most of these animals can be seen on the West Coast at a number of different sites, or at the aquarium in San Francisco, at Sea World in San Diego, or at Marine World in Petaluma, California. If travel to the West Coast is not possible, a trip to your library for books and videos is worthwhile. These sea animals are really interesting.

WAGONS HO

Visit the past on a trip in a covered wagon, and learn what the pioneer life was like. For information, write to:

Oregon Trail Wagon Train, Route 2, Box 502, Bayard, NE 69334

Wagons Ho Wagon Train, P.O. Box 60098, Phoenix, AZ 85082

ARCHEOLOGY DIG

 The archeology department of your local college or university can give you information about digs that you can go on; be sure to ask if a teenager can accompany you. Digs may be underway relatively close to home or in another country, are usually inexpensive and can have tax advantages. But you must be very interested, because as well as being fascinating, they are hard work. More information is also available from:

Elderhostel, 80 Boylston Street, Boston, MA 02116

WHITE WATER RAFTING

 An exciting adventure for you and your grandchildren is white water rafting. Trips are available that include a crew to help with camp set-up, gear and meals as well as river navigation. You'll have more fun than you had since *you* were a kid, and the kids will have a ball! Write for information:

> *National Association of Canoe Liveries and Outfitters (NACLO)*, P.O. Box 1149, Murdock, FL 33938

SCUBA DIVING

More and more people over 50 are taking up this fascinating sport, and we know the kids will love it. Find out more at your sporting goods store, and then plan a trip to a warm place, like Hawaii, to view the wonderful world under water.

WOODEN BOAT CAMP

If woodworking and boating are both right down your street, *WoodenBoat* in Brooklin, Maine, offers a wonderful week-long camp you can attend. Included are accommodations, food, and a wonderful workshop where you and your grandchild can produce your own small wooden boat, ready for you to launch and then take home at the end of one week's work. You and your grandchild can have a very special week together with a terrific pay-off at the end! Write for information.

> *WoodenBoat*, Box 78, Brooklin ME 04616

BACKPACKING AND CAMPING

 Getting away from normal life into the outdoors is a wonderful way to spend time with your grandchildren. They love sleeping and cooking outdoors, and have an opportunity to show you how able they are to help with collecting firewood, cooking, pitching tents and cleaning up the campsite at the end of your stay. Sitting around the campfire at night is the time for story-telling and sing-a-longs. Your reference librarian has a list of national campgrounds. You may need to call ahead to make a reservation.

Backpacker Magazine, CBS Magazines, 1515 Broadway, New York, NY 10036

Backpacker's Source Book, Penny Hargrove, Berkeley: Wilderness Press, 1987

CHARTER FISHING

 Plan a deep-sea fishing trip to one of the coastal communities that has charters available. Your travel agent can help you, and the Chamber of Commerce of the city you plan to visit also has lists of boat charters available.

STEAM TRAIN EXCURSION

 For an exciting old-fashioned train trip on the California Western Railroad, one of the most scenic shortlines in America, write to:

Pacific Locomotive Association/Key Tours, 1390 South Main Street, Suite 312, Walnut Creek, CA 94596

GO ON A LLAMA TREK

Both you and your grandchildren can have a unique experience llama trekking. This adventure is now available in many states and countries. A trek can range from a gourmet luncheon trek of ½ day to a week or longer. Your destination might be a lodge, or a bed and breakfast establishment, or tenting with sleeping bags in the wilderness. Most llama breeders are flexible, and will plan a trek to fit you. Llamas can carry up to

30% of their weight, so you don't have to carry your own gear, and children up to approximately 100 pounds can catch a ride when they become weary. Llamas are known to be gentle, good with children, curious, sure-footed, clean and odor-free, quiet (they "hum" on the trail), intelligent and patient.

For information about llama trekking near you, write to:

International Llama Association, P.O. Box 36505, Denver, CO 80237

THE ADVENTURE COMPANY

For fantastic adventures for the very active or the mildly-to-moderately active, this company can help you plan an African safari, a trek in the Scottish highlands, a trip to Machu Picchu and the Peruvian mountains or dozens of other exciting dream holidays that your older grandchildren would love to share. Here is what they say: "...discover new things about nature, this world and ourselves...in small parties...enjoying first-hand the boundless beauty and variety of our small planet." For their beautiful catalog, write to:

Mountain Travel, The Adventure Company, 6420 Fairmount Avenuye, El Cerrito, CA 94503